LITTLE ARTISTS HANDMADE

STOCKMAR
Nr. 1 Karminrot

Carly Schwerdt

VIKING
an imprint of
PENGUIN BOOKS

ACKNOWLEDGEMENTS

I would like to thank everyone who made this book possible, especially Jo for giving me the opportunity to create a book about something I loved, and for seeing that vision through to the last detail – including bringing the crew (Marley, Paul and Karen) to Nest Studio for a week of photo shoots. Thanks also to the creative team at Penguin (Claire and Hannah) who turned my words inside out and upside down to create a beautiful book. Big kisses to Amy for keeping not just the studio running smoothly, but my sanity – thank you for working tirelessly with me, I am forever grateful for your strength and your belief in me, I could never have finished with out you; Chris, for being such an awesome husband and dad, for taking care of our family and for always being there for me; Lily, for being a constant inspiration – this is your book sweetie; Olive, for her cuddles and her naps which gave me precious book-writing time; all the grandparents, for taking care of my girls when things got busy; Fiona, Tali, Claire, Michelle & Lisa, for always showing such great enthusiasm and support; the entire crafting community – without your keen interest this book would not be possible; all of the lovely Moopy & Me readers and Nest Studio visitors who have stopped for a chat, you guys rock! Your encouragement makes all of the hard work worthwhile. And finally, thanks to all of the children and families who have shared their love of art at Nest Studio over the years, I think you're all a bit brilliant!

Carly Schwerdt

ABOUT THE AUTHOR

Carly Schwerdt is an artist and textile designer who has contributed original projects to many modern craft anthologies. Carly lives and works in South Australia where she runs Nest Studio; an inspiring retail store and working design studio where she also teaches children's art classes.

To see more of Carly's work, visit her blog at **www.neststudio.typepad.com** or her store at **www.umbrellaprints.com.au**

CONTENTS

Screen Filler
Speedball
Speedball
junior + kindy paints
student + artist paints

ABOUT THIS BOOK

When my daughter Lily started drawing, I was utterly inspired by her work. Children's art is so raw and uninhibited; they create with a freedom of expression that adults can spend their entire lives trying to recapture. In the art classes I teach at Nest Studio, I see children creating masterpieces every day – this fuels my appetite for beautiful things and inspires me to create.

For Christmas a few years ago, I gave everyone in my extended family a lino print made from Lily's first attempt at drawing people. Everyone loved them! From that day forward, I was hooked. What started as a way to share Lily's art with our family has become an endless source of inspiration for my own work. There are days when I don't feel so confident with my own designs, but if I am working with my child's art then I know that what I am making is beautiful, fresh and completely unique.

This book is divided into two sections: the first contains art projects for your child, and the second has craft projects for you to make from their beautiful work. Each craft project includes a recommendation for which types of artwork from your child are particularly suitable, but in many cases you can easily adapt the project to suit any piece of art your child has made.

This book should leave you sure of two things: that your child's art is breathtaking, and that you can easily make something fabulous with it at home.

ART

INTRODUCTION

The relationship between art and children's cognitive growth is undeniable. Practising art stimulates the right side of the brain, helping kids develop spatial awareness, empathy, and the ability to understand abstract concepts and geometric principles. Art-making increases a child's understanding of visual and symbolic language, and teaches them to creatively problem-solve and to make choices with confidence. Painting a picture is all about subconscious decision-making. What do I want to paint? How do I paint a dog? What colour is it? Should I use a thick brush or a thin brush? How big is the dog? What shape is its head? But the best thing about all of this is that art is fun! Children rarely need any encouragement to pick up a pencil or to stick their hands in some paint.

The following art projects are designed to help children develop their practical art skills – as confidence grows, so does the opportunity for real creative expression, allowing for a richer, more satisfying art-making experience.

Getting started

The art component of this book is divided into three sections, each covering a different art-making method:

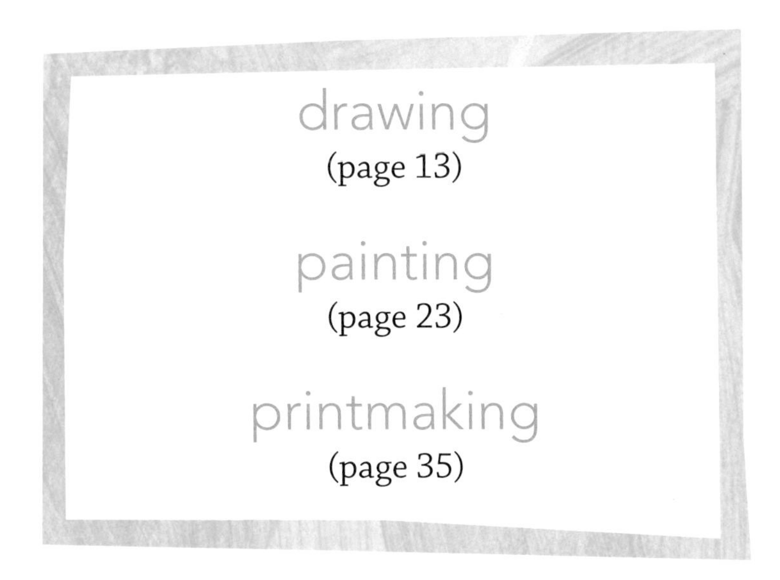

Each section contains projects designed to help children learn different ways to apply each art method. The projects are arranged in order of difficulty, so you can work your way through the book – or you can let your little one choose whichever project they feel like doing that day!

Materials

You never know when a child will have a burst of creativity, so it's important to have materials on hand. The following are the basic art materials I like to keep in the house at all times:

- a variety of types of paper – including coloured paper, large sheets of newsprint or butcher's paper, sketchbooks, thick watercolour paper and some nice drawing paper
- child-safe scissors
- coloured wax crayons
- soft grey-lead pencils
- coloured pencils or watercolour pencils
- pencil sharpener
- modelling clay or home-made playdough
- acrylic paint in yellow, red, blue, black and white
- paint brushes in a variety of sizes
- a box of mark-making materials – Lego, toy cars, rocks, sticks, kitchen sponges, forks, leaves, house-painting brushes, old toothbrushes and anything else you can think of that will roll, scrape, brush or stamp that can be washed and reused

I also have a bag full of hand towels and rags (which are washed up at the end of the week) to encourage cleaning up and to help keep mess to a minimum.

The projects in this book often require additional materials; these are listed on the first page of each project.

Quality is important

Although it may be tempting to buy cheap art supplies for your children, it is well worth building a collection of good-quality materials. Cheap materials usually lack good texture, vibrant colour and durability – which can make for a poor art-making experience. In the end, it's actually more cost-effective to teach your child how to look after quality art materials than to keep having to buy new things.

Organising materials

If it's possible, it's really helpful to create a workspace for your child. It doesn't have to be a whole room (although that would be lovely) – depending on the amount of space you have at home, you could have a corner dedicated to art making, a small table with a box of supplies underneath, or a low shelf or box to store art supplies that is close to the kitchen or dining-room table. The important thing is that materials are easily accessible so that kids can make art when the mood takes them.

It is also important to keep everything organised, and to introduce a routine for looking after materials and packing up. I have a few plastic crates for my daughter Lily's art supplies. Inside the crates, materials are stored in a variety of containers (mostly recycled items such as ice-cream containers, jars and shoe boxes). It helps kids keep things organised if the containers are clearly labelled – when Lily was little, I took photos of her things and then stuck the photos onto the boxes so that she knew where everything went.

LYRA FUN COLOUR

Feedback and analysis

When your child is making art, the emphasis should always be on the process and not the end result. Children should never be made to feel that there is a 'right' or 'wrong' way to depict something. However, there are definitely ways in which you can help your little one to think about what they are doing in order help them develop their skills. Positive feedback is extremely important, but it can become meaningless if it's not specific: before jumping to say how amazing your child's work is, stop and take notice of the composition, shapes and colours, and comment on what you see. For example, 'I can see how the blue stripes go right across the page', 'Look how these shapes are lining up together', and, 'I can see three different yellow colours. Wow! How did you make those?' This is a great way to help your child to build their observational skills and to start thinking about their art.

Ask your child questions about their artwork – what do they think of the picture? Why did they choose those particular colours? Are they pleased with the picture? Which parts were the most fun to create? Which were the hardest? Why?

The same approach can be taken when looking at the work of other artists. A discussion with your child about what they see in a piece of art is such a great way for them to learn how to appreciate, analyse, and, most importantly, develop their own opinions about art. When prompting discussion, try to choose artworks that your child will find relevant and interesting, as the key here is to instil a love of art and to have a stimulating dialogue – therefore, a fine example of Humanism in 16th-century Italian Renaissance painting is probably not the best place to start! I find picture books are an incredibly rich resource for teaching art – I use them all the time in the classes I teach at Nest Studio. These books are designed to engage children and so many of them are full of the most amazing art. Chances are, if you are looking at a book you've read together a number of times, your child will probably already have formed opinions about the artwork and will just need a little guidance and encouragement in order to express them.

Overcoming obstacles

Children often go through a difficult stage in their art making, when they try to emulate the work of artists they admire, or they start to think that a drawing or painting is meant to look as real as a photograph, and they end up getting frustrated by their lack of skills. Unfortunately, this can lead children to decide that they are no longer artists, and they will quite often want to quit art making altogether. Sadly, in my years of teaching, I have heard so many children express these feelings, with kids as young as four telling me, 'I am not a good drawer'.

There are plenty of things we can do to help kids overcome this lack of confidence – sometimes all that's needed is a bit of extra praise and encouragement. If that doesn't work, suggest that they try a new method of art making – if they don't like the way they paint, maybe they can have fun with some modelling clay, instead. And finally, I have found that using your child's artwork to create a piece of craft to be proudly displayed in your home, or given as a precious gift, provides an enormous confidence boost and can really help to get them excited about art again.

DRAWING

Introduction

There is no secret to drawing. As long as you can hold a pen, pencil, crayon, texta – anything that makes a mark – then you can draw!

A simple walk around the neighbourhood or backyard, or a cosy picture-book session can provide all the encouragement necessary to inspire a drawing activity. A tradition at our house, and maybe at yours too, is to have family drawing time – usually in the early morning when ideas are fresh; or in quiet times before bed or before the evening meal. We have paper and pencils at the ready in the buffet next to the dining-room table so that we are ready whenever the inclination arises.

The following drawing activities are fairly unstructured and are great for developing observation skills and hand–eye coordination.

Line and mark-making

If you take a good look at any drawing, no matter how simple or complex, you can see that it is made up of just a few different types of marks – straight lines, curvy lines, dots and shading – all of which are really just different types of line. It is the materials used and the way the lines are made that allow you to create shape and texture and to express a feeling or an idea.

Shape

Line can be used to create shapes that describe an object, or to make shapes that are completely abstract.The simplest way to draw a shape is to make a line where the end meets up with the beginning. Learning to draw shapes is one of the most important steps in a child's early education, as it provides the foundation of literacy and mathematics. The ability to recognise a shape and copy it is really the key to being able to form letters, so young children who are confident drawers are extremely well equipped when it comes to learning to write.

Texture

Texture in drawing is the creation of a sense of the physical properties of a surface; for example, making something look smooth, rough or hairy. A nice way to create texture in a drawing is to repeat a similar type of line or shape. Take a really close look at the illustrations in a story book the next time your family has some reading time – notice how a furry texture is created using a whole lot of lines going in a similar direction, or the way lots and lots of dots close together can look like dirt or sand.

Expression

Mark-making is really the basis for all visual communication and you can express an enormous amount with very little. The shape and direction of a line can vividly represent emotion: an upwardly curving line depicts a smile, an expression of happiness; turn the same line upside-down and you have sadness. A ziz-zagging line might represent anger, or dynamic movement, or something spiky; whereas a curvy line is more likely to represent something smooth and calm.

Children usually start their art-making at a young age with the humble scribble and, while the above ideas are good to know about, it is also important that kids are able to develop their art skills at a pace that comes naturally to them. Let your child draw what they want, then chat with them about how they made the marks on the page: 'Look, you pressed really hard with the pencil and it made a dark line.'

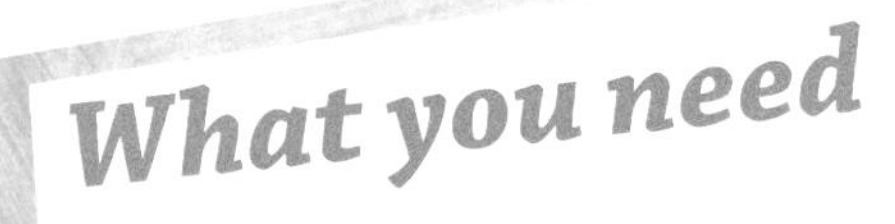

What you need

- black pen or texta
- coloured pencils, watercolour pencils or crayons
- paper or a sketchbook

tips + tricks

With older children, you can try discussing what art techniques they think were used to make the illustrations in the book and what it is they like about the style of the pictures. This helps to develop observation and analysis skills, and can help kids think about what styles of art they like most.

PICTURE BOOKS

What to do

Encouraging children to use books for inspiration is one of my favourite art-teaching methods. Children can relate to the beautiful artworks in picture books through story and familiarity, and the tactile nature of books make them instantly more engaging than a painting in an art gallery. Grab an armful of your family's most beloved books and look through them together. See which colours, characters and drawing techniques grab your child's attention, and start their drawing from there.

One of our all-time family favourites is *Mrs Armitage Queen of the Road*, by Quentin Blake. After Lily and I read this story together, she was really interested in the idea of drawing her own car with lots of fun gadgets attached. This inspired the drawing pictured to the left. Lily drew whatever her heart desired and I encouraged her to think about where the car and road were in relation to the trees and the sky, and how she thought she might make the car look shiny and the trees bushy. In this way, I was able to help her to think about how to create perspective and texture in her drawing.

I suggest using a pen or texta for this activity, rather than a pencil – it's a great way to encourage children to draw more freely. If you can't erase 'wrong' lines, then all lines have to be used somehow. This can be frustrating for them in the beginning, but with practice it helps little artists develop into free, creative thinkers. That unwanted wonky line can start to look like a little dog running along and that splodgy shape might look a bit like a face . . . A little encouragement teaches children to make the best of what they have, and they are usually happy to do so.

tips + tricks

The length of time spent drawing will really depend on your child and their age. Young children may not want to spend very long on one activity – 5 minutes is quite an achievement for kindergarten-aged children – but then again, your child may be engaged for over half an hour. The point is, any amount of time is wonderful for hand-eye coordination as well as line-work practice.

ANIMALS

What to do

Animals are such wonderful things to draw – they come in so many different shapes, sizes, colours and textures. An animal might be small, smooth and scaly, or big, spotted and furry. Kids can draw animals they know or make up amazing new creatures.

Given the right kind of day, you should be able to find an animal to look at from your own backyard or balcony, a park or school playground – it could be a family pet, an ant colony found on a hot sunny day or some snails and worms wriggling about in the garden. If you can't find any animals, or if it's too cold to go outside, curl up in a cosy corner with some books on animals from your library.

For this project Lily and I spent some time outside chatting to the cockatoos in our walnut tree and to Oscar, our family's dog. Drawing real-life animals that don't sit still can be a challenge – I find that encouraging quick sketching makes this a lot easier and can really help kids learn to draw more freely. Younger children will probably still draw from their memory and imagination, but you can ask them questions about the animal they're drawing to get them to notice a few extra details – for example, Lily noticed how floppy Oscar's ears were and that his collar was red.

What you need

- sketchbook or loose sheets of paper on a clipboard
- 2B pencil or texta
- coloured pencils or crayons

STILL LIFE

What to do

Drawing from life is a great way for children to practise observation and to learn to recognise shape, line and texture. Set up a still life on your kitchen table. This can be anything you like – maybe a vase filled with some flowers or leaves, or some fruit sitting in a bowl.

We have some lovely flowers growing in our garden at certain times of the year. There often aren't enough of the one kind for a full bunch, so I picked different types and popped them into a water glass for Lily to draw – the variety of colours and sizes made for a really interesting drawing experience.

There's no right or wrong way for your child to draw what they see and you should always resist the urge to tell them how something should look – instead, ask simple questions as a way of giving your child guidance and getting them to really look at and think about the object they're drawing. What kinds of shapes can you see? Are they spiky leaves or round? What colours do you think you should use?

What you need

- 2B pencil
- coloured pencils, watercolour pencils or crayons
- drawing paper or sketchbook
- soft paintbrush and cup of water (if using watercolour pencils)
- items to make your still life

tips + tricks

Young children will often be finished with this activity before you can even make yourself a cup of tea. Why not ask them if they would like to search their room for objects to draw – a favourite toy or five will make for an enthusiastic artist! And you may even get that cuppa . . .

PAINTING

Introduction

Kids love painting – it's fun, unpredictable and full of surprises, and the swirling colours and opportunities to experiment are irresistible. Children can paint with a brush or just a finger – or a sponge, or a stick, or almost anything for that matter. Even the most basic forms of painting will, in time, give children the skills they need to control the paint; allowing them a freedom of expression not always possible with pencils. Put on some fun music to paint to and let your child go crazy!

Undeniably, painting is a messy activity – but don't let that scare you off. It's easy to set some boundaries; you could cover everything in sight with newspaper, or let your kids paint in the backyard in the nude, so they can be hosed off afterwards. Showing children how to clean up their brushes and palettes can be fun, and it teaches them to value and look after their art materials. You can minimise mess by only putting out a little bit of paint at a time. It's always best to have too little than too much, as there's less waste and less paint to go on the walls and the floor and table and the face and wherever else takes your child's fancy. If you do have left over paint, rather than wash it down the sink, use it to paint scrap paper. Once it's dry you can use it for collage, pretty notepaper – whatever you like!

Colour theory

Knowing just a few important things about colour theory makes mixing paint so much easier, making the process of painting more enjoyable and expressive. A colour wheel is a wonderful tool for learning about colours – they're available from art-supply shops, or you can just make your own.

Primary, secondary and tertiary colours

Primary colours are colours that can't be created by mixing other colours together. The three primary colours are red, blue and yellow. Secondary colours are made by mixing two primary colours together. For example, if you mix red and blue together you get purple. The three secondary colours are purple, green and orange. Tertiary colours are the colours in between the primary colours and the secondary colours. For example if you mix yellow and orange together you get yellow-orange.

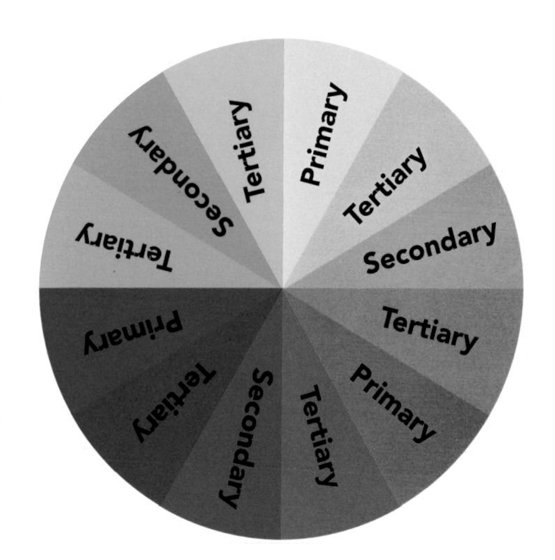

Tint and shade

Tint and shade refer to the lightness or darkness of a colour. Mix white paint into your colour to make a light tint, or mix in black paint to mark a dark shade.

Warm and cool colours

Recognising whether a colour is cool or warm is more about the feeling you get from a colour rather than any strict rules; while warm colours are often based around yellows and reds, and cold colours around blues and greens, you can still have a cool yellow or a warm blue. Warm colours are usually bright, bold and happy, and will really stand out in a painting; while cool colours are more calm and soothing, and will stand out less than warm colours.

The best way to learn about colours is to play and to practise! A great exercise is for kids to find colours they really like – it might be the green of a leaf or the pink of a favourite stuffed toy – and to try to match the colours by mixing their paints.

WATERCOLOURS

Watercolour paints are fabulous – the colours are bright and translucent, and it's a pleasure to watch them melt into each other as they spread across the page. They are also a great deal less messy to use than acrylic paints – solid watercolour paints are used straight from their neat little boxes and liquid paints can be mixed in small glass jars on a tray. And the best part? Good-quality solid watercolour paints are simply left to dry for next time, which means no waste and all you have to wash are your brushes!

What you need

- art smock (page 111)
- box of solid watercolour paints
- watercolour brushes (two sizes at least)
- paper (thick watercolour paper is best)
- pencil, waterproof marker or crayon
- cups or jars for water
- newspaper
- paper towel

What to do

1. Before any painting session, you should cover your work surface with lots of newspaper. Watercolour painting is best done on a table or other flat surface. If you use an easel, the paint tends to run down the page – which can look lovely, but can also be frustrating to little artists if it's not the effect they want.

2. Make a sketch on the watercolour paper with a 2B pencil, waterproof marker, or crayon (the wax in crayons can actually be really helpful, particularly for younger artists, as it forms a water-proof barrier that keeps the paint from running all over the page). Until children are confident with watercolour paints, I find that the most successful sessions start with a drawing. Having an outline to colour in allows kids to experiment with the paint and colours more confidently, as they're not so worried about trying to form shapes and lines – which can be tricky when starting out with watercolours.

3. Once the drawing is done, set out the paints and brushes. You'll need at least two jars of water – one for rinsing brushes and one for clean water (you may need to change the clean water a few times during a session).

4. When it's time to paint, there's no need for too many instructions. The most basic watercolour painting technique is to dip the brush into the clean water, smoosh it around a little on the paint, and then put the brush to paper. When you want to change colours, rinse the brush in the rinsing water, then dip it into the clean water and off you go again! One thing you might want to help your little artist with is brushstroke, as watercolours work best with a light touch. Glide the brush over the paper only once or twice in the same spot – working the paint too much will rub into the paper and maybe even create a hole. A piece of paper towel can be handy for soaking up puddles.

5. When your little one is done painting, put their masterpiece aside to dry. To clean up the paint box, just mop up any water with some paper towel, brush over the paints with fresh water and dab dry with some more paper towel.

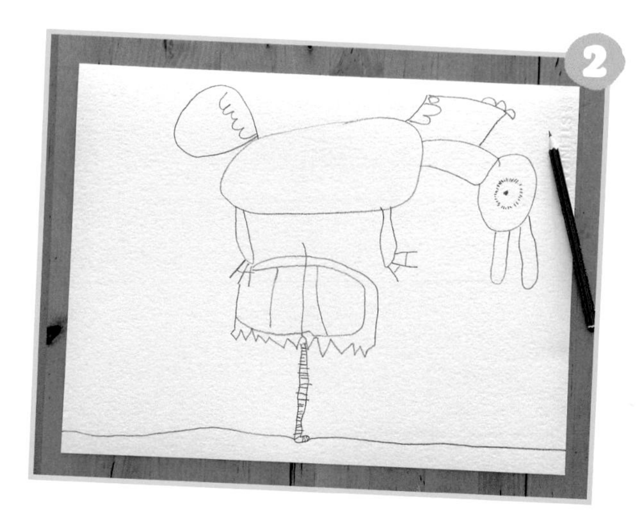

tips + tricks

When your little artist is more confident using watercolours, you can help them experiment with some techniques. Vary the amount of water they use on the brush – how different does the paint look when they only use a tiny bit of water? Blob some clean water onto the page, and then add some paint to that. Try holding the brush above the page and allowing the paint to drip and spread by itself. There are so many fun ways to experiment with watercolours!

ACRYLICS

This project is a really fun way to get kids to try an approach to art that, rather than just being about creating freely, involves a little bit of thought and planning, as it needs to be done in stages. The project also functions as a natural lesson in composition, as planning the stages are essentially about identifying which colours and shapes belong in the background, middleground and foreground.

Completing this activity can take up to three or more sessions, as layers of paint need to dry between sittings. Hot weather or a hairdryer can speed this up for keen little artists.

What you need

- art smock (page 111)
- stretched canvas
- paper (optional)
- 2B pencil
- newspaper
- acrylic paints
- paint brushes (two sizes at least)
- ice-cream container lids (or similar) for mixing paint
- cups or jars for water

What to do

1. Start with a sketch. You can draw directly onto the canvas with a pencil, or onto a separate piece of paper so you have a guide to refer to as you build up your painting. As you can see in the picture above, Lily started with a sketch of a whale swimming in the ocean.

2. The first painting step is to paint the background. Lily's background layer was light blue for the sky. We mixed a little white paint into the primary blue, and also a little bit of water (this helps the paint to spread across a large area and the thinner paint can allow the sketch to show through). Encourage your little one to mix their own colours and paint right to the edges so that the whole canvas is covered.

3. Once the background layer is dry, help your child identify which of the elements from their drawing are in the middleground. Lily figured out that the middleground elements in her drawing were the water and the clouds, so she used white and blue paint to fill in these details. You can thin the paint with water again if you like, but only a little, as it needs to go over the background colour.

4. It should be pretty easy for kids to identify which elements of their drawing are in the foreground, as it's generally the main subject of their picture. In Lily's case, this is the whale. Make sure the paint is nice and thick for this top layer, so that it goes over the other layers easily without too much background colour showing through.

5. Three layers of paint is a good number to start with, but for kids who don't mind the in-between paint-drying stages, there's no reason to stop at three – they can paint as many layers as they like!

tips + tricks
While acrylic paint is water soluble, the pigments can still stain clothing and surfaces, so make sure everyone's dressed in old clothes or lovely art smocks, and cover all surfaces with newspaper before you begin.

PRINTMAKING

Introduction

The creative approach required for printmaking can be very different to that of drawing and painting. There are many different styles of print-making, but all require the creation of a surface for the print to be taken from (such as a screen, plate, or stencil). When making this surface, you need to imagine what the print will look like, so it involves a bit of fore-thought, planning and patience.

There are some special tools required for printmaking, and kids will need to learn how to use them and look after them. I find this aspect really adds to the appeal of printmaking for kids – it helps them feel like respon-sible artists.

Once all the hard work has gone into creating an inking plate or sten-cil, the magic really begins! Children love the repetition of printing; their designs can be created over and over – one in red, one in blue, one for my teacher, one for Grandma, one for Dad . . .

Composition

Children's art is so fascinating and interesting to look at, as they are unconscious of any expectations; they create, free from judgement. The lines children make are not as random as they appear; the child is telling a story, remembering an object, sharing a feeling, or just enjoying the process – how it looks and feels as the line runs across the page, how the colour fills up a space and then stops, takes a breath, and then starts all over again. Sooner or later, though, children start to become self-conscious about their art – creating less freely and more thoughtfully. When that time comes, being able to recognise and use some of the principles of design can really help them appreciate and enjoy the art-making process.

Contrast and harmony

Contrast can be best described as seeing and creating difference: small versus big, corner versus curve, blank versus busy, light versus dark, and so on. Harmony is seeing and creating similarities, often achieved by the repetition of shapes, textures and colours. Contrast and harmony working together in a piece of art creates visual interest and a sense of balance.

Positive and negative space

Positive space is the shape made by the subject of an image. Negative space is the shape made by the space around the subject. The screen printing project on page 47 is really great for learning about negative space – encourage your child to make a number of prints, moving the stencil to a different place on the screen each time (which will change the shape of the negative space) and then you can discuss how that alters the overall effect of the picture.

Movement

Movement is the way the arrangement of elements in an artwork makes your eye travel around the composition. Your eye will first notice the most dominating feature – be that the largest, darkest, brightest or busiest – and then move on through the spaces in between the next object, line or colour until it rests in a nice breathing space or continues to go around and around.

MAX

MONOPRINTING

Unlike most methods of printmaking, monoprinting doesn't allow for reproduction – you get just a single unique print. The charm of monoprinting comes from the delightful texture the method creates; it has a beautiful vintage feel and looks particularly lovely coloured with some pencils or watercolour paints.

This method of printing takes only a few minutes and is best done quickly (before the ink dries out too much). Keeping the drawing small helps make a successful print. Because of the speed in which these prints need to be created this is a great project for loosening up cautious drawers!

Young children might need help rolling the ink out at the start, but otherwise this is a really easy and fun project.

What you need

- water-based printing ink
- large plastic sheet (such as perspex or polypropylene)
- butter knife
- roller
- pencil
- paper

What to do

1. Place the plastic sheet on a flat surface. Put a grape-sized blob of ink in the middle, and smooth it flat with a butter knife.

2. Roll the ink gently away from you in an up and down motion, until the ink has spread to the width of the roller. Now roll the ink in a left and right motion.

3. Alternate between rolling up and down, and left and right, until the sheet is covered with a smooth, thin layer of ink.

4. Gently place a sheet of paper over the ink. Now you can start drawing! You can use any kind of pencil, but remember to hold it upright in your hand, so that you don't touch or lean on the paper – if you do, it will leave blotches of ink on the paper (although, this can make for a nice texture).

5. Carefully peel back the paper and there it is – a monoprint!

tips + tricks
If the monoprint is blotchy, either the ink wasn't spread thinly enough, or you've leaned on the paper. If it's difficult to peel the paper off, then you've probably spent a little too long doing the drawing and the ink has started to dry.

FAUX LINO PRINTING

The idea for this art project came out of pure necessity; lino printing produces beautiful results, but the cutting tools are far too sharp and dangerous for little hands. So, I designed a fun and safe method that uses pencils and craft foam instead. Young children might need a little help inking the craft foam, but otherwise this is suitable for artists of all ages.

The foam printing plates can be washed and used time and time again – try printing with new colours or adding more grooves to the foam.

What you need

- craft foam
- sharp pencil
- texta (optional)
- scissors
- water-based printing ink
- large plastic sheet (such as perspex or polypropylene)
- roller
- paper
- metal spoon

What to do

1. With a sharp pencil, scratch an illustration into the sheet of craft foam. (I find it's easier to draw the picture onto the foam first in texta, then scratch over the lines with the pencil.) Make sure that the grooves are scratched deeply into the foam (you may need to go over them a few times). You may also like to cut the foam into a shape after you've made your illustration – Lily cut around the outline of her drawing, but you can cut it into any shape you like.

2. Now you need to get your ink rolled out nice and smooth so that you get a thin, even coverage on the roller. Do this by following steps 1–3 for Monoprinting (page 41).

3. Once the roller is evenly coated, gently roll it over the foam until the foam is evenly covered with ink. The foam may want to stick to your roller so make sure you hold it flat while you are rolling (a few extra fingers from Mum or Dad can be a real help). Your scratched grooves shouldn't have any ink in them – if they do, you probably have a bit too much ink on your roller, or your grooves may not be deep enough.

4. Lay a sheet of paper on a clean flat surface. Carefully place the inked foam face down onto the paper and gently smooth it flat. With the back of a

spoon, rub the foam in circular motions, pressing it firmly into the paper. Make sure you do this all over.

5. Gently lift one corner of the foam away from the paper and peel it back, being careful not to smudge your print (it can help to hold the opposite end of the foam down as you do this).

tips + tricks

You can make as many prints as you like using your foam template. Try covering a huge piece of paper with lots and lots of prints, or building up a picture by layering different colours – simply wash the foam and the plastic sheet and start again with a new colour.

SCREEN PRINTING

Screen printing with paper stencils can produce results that look just as good as prints made using professional methods. I often use this technique myself when testing out ideas for fabrics, and it's great for making printed calico bags, tea towels and t-shirts.

Making stencils and screen printing is a fabulous way for children to learn about positive and negative shape recognition, spatial relationships and problem solving.

Screen printing involves using a few different tools and requires a bit of setting up, so your little one will probably need a bit of assistance. However, older kids should be able to do most of this on their own after they've done it a few times with an adult.

What you need

- tracing paper
- iron
- 2B pencil
- scissors
- craft knife (optional)
- old fabric or newspaper
- paper or fabric for printing onto
- silk screen
- masking tape
- water-based printing ink
- butter knife or spoon
- squeegee

What to do

1. Tear off a few pieces of tracing paper and press with an iron on low heat to flatten them out (Mum or Dad might need to do this). Using a pencil, draw the stencil design on the tracing paper. Large, strong shapes work best, and keep in mind that the pictures need to be cut out, so you don't want them to be too fiddly. Dinosaurs are a very popular screen-printing subject in my house – you can't help but draw them big and bold!

2. Plan which parts of the stencil will be positive shapes and which parts will be negative shapes. Wherever there is a hole in the stencil, the ink will pass through and make colour on the paper or fabric – so the negative shape in your stencil will be the positive (coloured) shape in your print. It can be a good idea to start with a solid shape, if this is your first time screen printing, and then work your way up to more complicated designs. Cut out the stencil using a pair of scissors. You can cut bits out of the inside of a shape by slightly folding the paper and cutting a snip in the fold. Then slide your scissors into that little snip to cut out the shape (sticky tape can be very handy to tape up accidental cuts). If the design is really complicated and has bits that are too fiddly for scissors, then an adult can cut out those pieces with a craft knife.

tips + tricks

You can make a positive-shape stencil, which results in a print with a coloured background and your stencil shape in white, or you can cut negative shapes into a sheet of paper (as pictured), which results in a print with a plain background and your stencil shapes in colour.

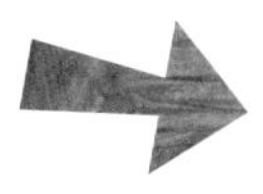

What to do continued

3. Mask the edges of the screen with masking tape. The ink won't pass through the tape, so, if you are using a positive-shape stencil, this will create the edges of your print. Cover your workspace with old fabric or newspaper and place your printing surface (this could be paper or fabric or whatever you like – just make sure that your ink is suitable) on top. Place your stencil on your printing surface and put the screen over the top.

4. Using a butter knife, spread a generous amount of ink in a line across the top of the masking-taped part of the screen or, if your print is going to be small, spread a thin line of ink onto the blade of the squeegee. Now place the squeegee blade onto the screen above the ink and pull it firmly down the screen towards you, holding the squeegee at a 45-degree angle. Little artists will need to use both hands to pull the squeegee, so they'll need a helper to hold the screen in place.

5. Hold the printing surface down and carefully lift the screen off (the ink should make the stencil stick to the screen). If you're not making another print straight away, wash your screen immediately to prevent dried ink from clogging the holes and ruining your screen. Once your print is dry, you can add new colours or more prints on top to create a layered effect.

tips + tricks

If you are printing onto fabric, allow the ink to dry, then go over it for a good five minutes with a hot iron – this sets the ink so it won't come out in the wash.

GOCCO PRINTING

Print Gocco is a home screen-printing system developed in Japan. It is a brilliant contraption that lets you create highly-detailed printing screens, perfect for reproducing drawings. The downside to the Gocco is its small size and expensive consumables (two print lamps are needed every time you make a screen). However, the unique results are definitely worth the expense!

The Gocco printer is probably a bit tricky for small children to use on their own, so it can be best for adults to make the screen with the little one looking on. Let them take over when it comes time to print.

You need to use a photocopier or laser printer to create your image for use in the Print Gocco, as it's the carbon in the toner which allows the machine to work.

What you need

- Print Gocco machine
- scrap paper
- photocopy (or a black and white laser printer copy) of your favourite drawing, trimmed to 10 cm × 15 cm (4 in × 6 in)
- 2 × Gocco print lamps
- Hi-Mesh screen
- old fabric or newspaper
- paper or fabric for printing onto
- small squeegee
- water-based printing ink

What to do

1. Open up your Print Gocco machine. Put a piece of scrap paper over the rubber pad and then place your photocopy on top, facing up. Put the Hi-Mesh screen into place (check the manufacturer's instructions – the method varies between different models of Gocco printer). Close the lid, and make sure your photocopied image is in the right place (you'll be able to see it through the clear panel in the lid).

2. Screw the globes into the lamp housing, making sure they are firmly in place. Slot the lamp housing into the Gocco lid, lining up the arrows. With hands on either side of the handle, press down very firmly with both hands and hold for 3–4 seconds – you will see and hear the bulbs flashing and crackling. Don't look directly at the machine while you do this, as the bulbs are very bright.

3. Remove the lamp housing from the lid (don't touch the bulbs as they get very hot) and set aside. Open up the Gocco machine and you will see your photocopy stuck to the Hi-Mesh screen. Take the screen out and gently peel off the paper.

4. Cover your work surface with old fabric or newspaper and place your printing surface (this could be paper or fabric or whatever you like – just make sure that your ink is suitable) on top. Place the screen on top.

1

3

4

What to do *continued*

5. Smear some ink along your squeegee blade with a butter knife and then pull the squeegee firmly down the screen towards you, holding the squeegee at a 45-degree angle. You should only have to make one pass with the ink – all it takes is a bit of practice to get the feel for it and you'll be making perfect prints every time!

5

6. Hold your printing surface down and carefully lift the screen off. If you're not making another print straight away, wash your screen immediately to prevent dried ink from clogging the holes and ruining your screen. Once your print is dry you can add new colours or more prints on top to create a layered effect. If you are printing onto fabric, allow the ink to dry, then go over it with a hot iron for a good five minutes – this sets the ink so it won't come out in the wash.

6

tips + tricks
If your print is too blotchy, either your ink is too dry, or you need to be more firm and even with your squeegee. Keep practising and try thinning the ink with a bit of water. If your print has bleed marks, the fabric may have moved, is wrinkly or you pulled too hard. The ink could also be too wet – if so, leave the ink out for a while to dry out a little.

CRAFT

INTRODUCTION

The following craft projects provide detailed step-by step instructions, but they're also intended as a source of inspiration, so are completely open to your interpretation. If the instructions say to embroider some felt onto a bag and you feel like screen printing, then go right ahead! Most of the ideas can be interchanged between mediums, materials and methods. Making the projects relevant to your child and their artwork is what's most important, as it will keep them interested and passionate about their work as well as validate their ideas.

Getting started

Before you start on any of the following craft projects, here are a few general things to note:

- wash and iron all fabrics before use
- when tracing templates onto tracing paper, be sure to transfer all markings
- the use of any small parts – such as buttons or googly eyes – to decorate toys will make them unsuitable for children under three years of age. If the toy is for a small child, use embroidery or appliqué to decorate instead.

Don't forget
1m fabric
buttons
threads
watercolour brushes
lovely paper
glue
gocco bulbs
ink

Children in the craft space

It can be really hard to find the time to get any crafting done when you have children, as it can seem very impractical – and potentially dangerous – to have little ones around while you are working on a project. However, it is definitely possible to have children with you in your craft space; it just takes a little planning to help things run smoothly.

First of all, I always make sure the kids are well fed and well rested before I make a start on anything – you won't believe how much of a difference this will make! Small or sharp items such as needles, pins, scissors and buttons need to be stored in closable containers and kept out of reach of children. Toxic or otherwise dangerous craft supplies such as varnish and glue also need to be kept well out of your child's reach, or in a locked cupboard.

Once your space is child-proofed, you just have to give your kids something to do. Lily is five, so she's happy to get out her sewing kit and plan her own project (with a bit of help from me with threading needles and pinning patterns). When she tires of that she'll usually get out some paper and pencils. Olive is one, so she just needs a basket of toys and she'll play happily at my feet for almost an hour.

Child-friendly craft sessions are not always the most productive, so keep to simple projects, sorting out materials, a bit of embroidery or cutting out fabric rather than trying to finish a quilt or make a start on a complex garment.

Making a digital copy of your child's artwork

Once you have a copy of your child's artwork on your computer, you'll find that there's no end to the wonderful creative things you can do! If you have a scanner, you can use that to make a digital copy. However, if you don't have a scanner, or your child's art is too big to scan, you can just take a digital photo of it. When taking photos, make sure the camera is square to the artwork (and not on an angle), otherwise the image will be distorted. You will need to turn the flash off and find a place with nice even light to take the picture – this helps avoid glary hotspots on the photo.

Once you have uploaded your image to the computer, open it up in a picture-editing program such as Photoshop, Paint or Picnik. You can then crop out unwanted background; change the size; or tweak the colours, brightness and contrast, if necessary.

Transfers

When using an iron-on transfer or a transfer pencil, you will notice that the transferred picture ends up as a mirror-image of the original. This may not matter too much, but if you need to transfer some text or just want your transfer to be facing the right way around, all you need to do is flip the original image. Open the image in a picture-editing program and flip on the horizontal axis (this option will most likely be in a menu named 'Image'). Now you can print your transfer, or print a copy of the flipped image to trace with a transfer pencil.

Basic craft kit

There is no end to the materials and tools you can collect for crafting – believe me, I know! Here are a few essentials, which, together with the basic sewing kit on the following page, should get you through most of the projects in this book:

- scissors
- craft glue
- craft knife
- safety pins
- pencils and markers
- transfer pencil
- tracing paper
- polyester stuffing
- knitting needles
- computer and printer
- paper and cardboard in a range of colours and sizes
- assortment of buttons, beads, ribbons, felt pieces and fabric scraps.

Sewing basics

Basic sewing kit

Here are the materials you'll need for a basic sewing kit:

- sewing machine
- spare sewing-machine needles
- pins
- hand-sewing needles in various sizes
- sewing thread in a variety of colours
- embroidery needles
- embroidery thread in a variety of colours
- tape measure
- unpicker
- tailor's chalk
- scissors
- fabric scissors
- iron and ironing board.

I always keep a supply of notions in my sewing kit as well – things like buttons, press-studs, zips, twill tape, hooks and eyes, and elastic – they always come in handy.

You can keep your supplies in a special sewing organiser, but a toolbox or tackle box will do just as well.

Setting up

In an ideal world, you would have your sewing machine set up at all times in your lovely tidy craft room with all of your supplies neatly arranged and an ironing board and iron at the ready – but for most of us this just isn't practical or possible given limited space. All you really need is a table for your sewing machine in your kitchen or dining room, and if it's not big enough for laying out fabric you can use the floor (just watch out for kids or pets who seem to love nothing more than trying to play with your neatly arranged material!). I find it always makes a project run more smoothly if I set everything up within easy reach before I start, including the iron and ironing board, fabric scissors and pins by the sewing machine, and a little bowl or bin to collect the fabric scraps and threads.

Choosing fabric

My favourite part of planning a craft project is deciding which fabric to use. I tend to buy fabric well before I have a project in mind, falling in love with a pattern or colour combination. Any crafter will tell you that choosing fabric can be dangerously addictive and that addiction usually results in a huge stash of lovely fabric, just waiting for the right project to come along!

When choosing fabric combinations, I like to use colours and patterns that complement each other rather than match, such as a tiny repeat of flowers married with stripes, or little polka-dots paired with something bold and oversized.

Since fabric comes in such a wide variety of styles, textures, patterns and weights, it's important to select the right type. For the projects in this book, I recommend using medium-weight fabrics made from natural fibres such as cotton, linen and hemp. For printing in particular, I highly recommend using fabrics made from 100 per cent natural fibre, as a lot of inks won't set properly on synthetic fabric. If you're not sure about your ink or your fabric, you should do a test by dabbing some ink onto the fabric and seeing how it dries.

In my studio I prefer to use hemp–cotton blends, as the inks take well and the texture of the fabric is brilliant for sewing. Because hemp is such a strong fibre, its versatility is endless – it's durable enough to use for toys and upholstery, but also soft enough for making clothing.

Cutting templates and fabric

You can resize any of the templates in the back of the book to suit your need, except for the clothing patterns. For example, if you would like a large floor cushion rather than a little pillow, simply enlarge the Patchwork Cushion template (page 228) by 300 per cent.

When folding fabric, make sure the selvedges are lined up nice and straight. The selvedge is the non-fraying edge (it's often plain or a different colour to the rest of the fabric). The grain of the fabric runs parallel to the selvedge and the crosswise grain runs perpendicular. When laying your templates out on the fabric, make sure any straight edges are either placed on the fold of the fabric as indicated on the template, or are in line with the grain.

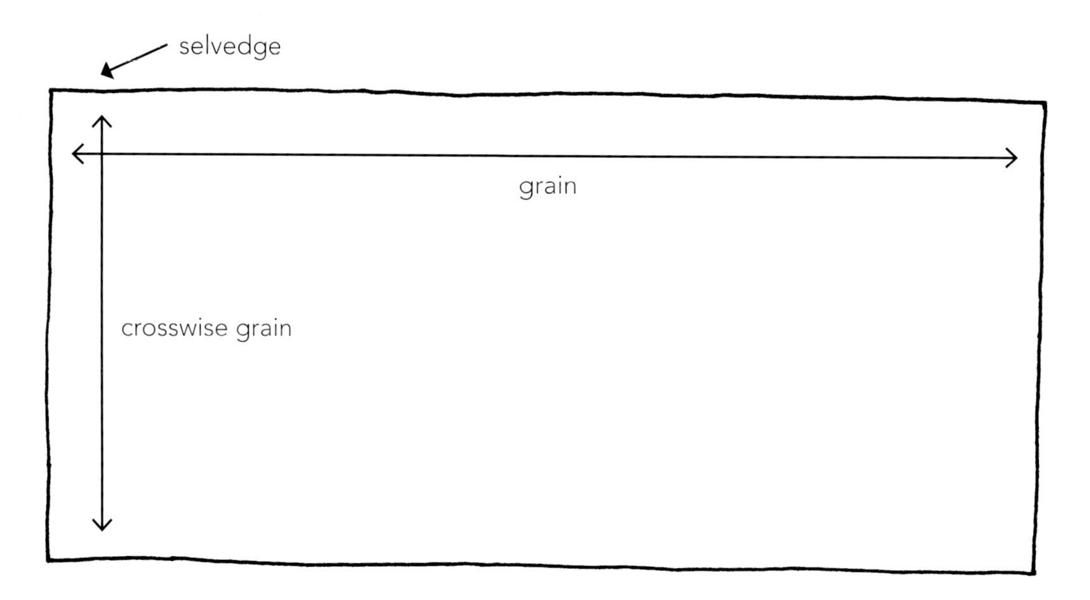

All of the templates include a seam allowance, but I generally cut out fabric slightly larger than is required, just in case! I would rather trim off excess than end up with something too small.

Stitch guide

When hand sewing, I really only use four kinds of stitch. The following should see that all of your sewing needs are met.

Straight stitch

The most simple stitch of all; made of evenly sized and spaced stitches, a straight stitch is a great utility stitch (for sewing things together) and should look like a dashed or broken line.

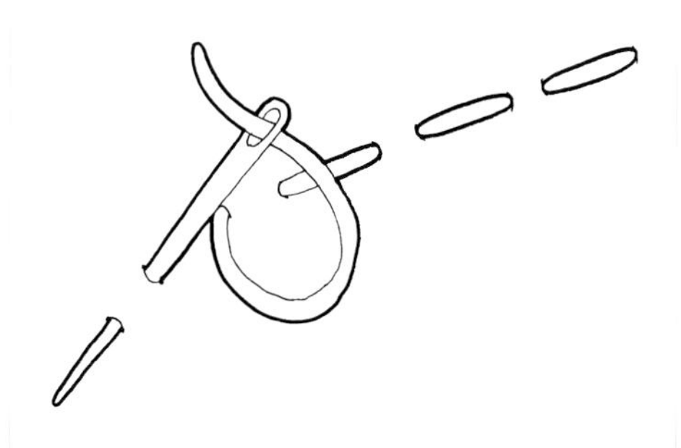

Back stitch

A nice simple stitch most commonly used for embroidering lines. The stitches are made backward to the direction you are sewing, and should look like an unbroken line (like a line of machine stitching). Backstitch is also a good utility stitch.

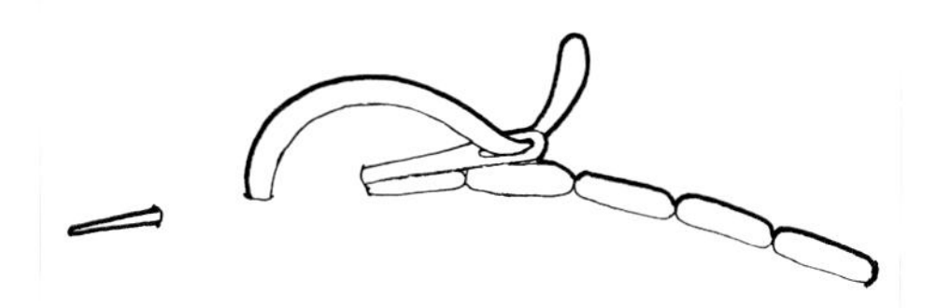

Ladder stitch

A ladder stitch is used for joining fabric edges together, so it's perfect for stitching up a hole left for stuffing or turning right way out. The stitches should be almost invisible.

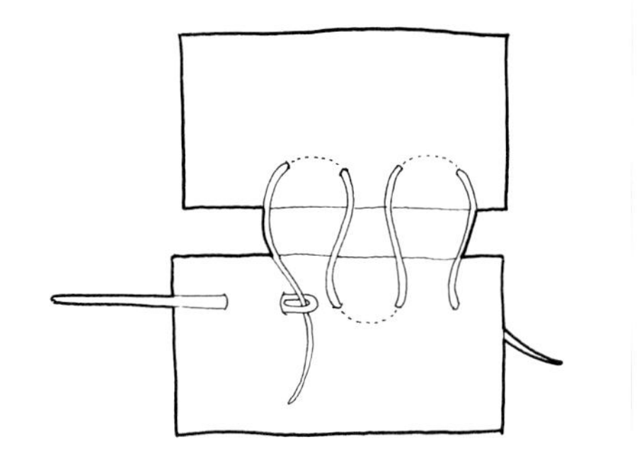

Blanket stitch

A blanket stitch is used for neatening edges and for decoration. Great for appliqué and for decorative edges on felt shapes. Use wool or embroidery thread in a contrasting colour.

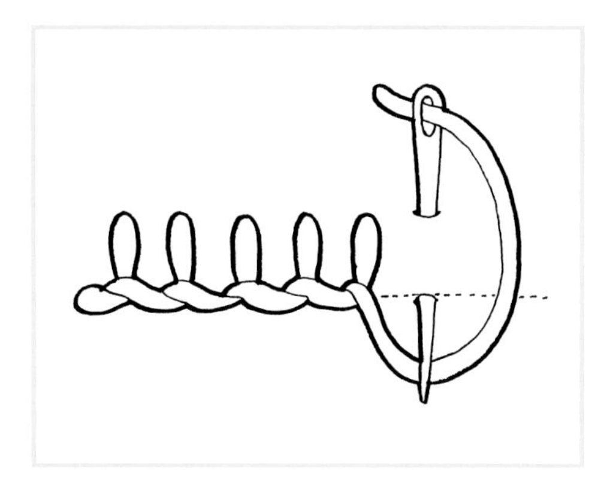

Machine stitching

I often use my sewing machine for embroidery, particularly if I'm in a hurry. A lot of modern machines allow you to do some incredibly detailed embroidery with the mere press of a button, but you'd be surprised by what you can achieve with a simple straight stitch. You can get a specific foot for free-motion sewing, but I just run my machine manually to control the stitches – it's a lot like drawing, but with a sewing machine instead of a pencil!

Finishing up

Once you've finished a sewing project, remember to snip off the loose threads, as they can tickle and can also get caught in the wash. I always like to give things an iron; to get rid of wrinkles and to press seams flat. Also, make sure any stuffing openings are neatly sewn up.

FOR KIDS

These adorable toys make great gifts, and are so quick to sew; you can easily make ten in one afternoon – give one to every child you know! You can use any piece of art for this project – I used Lily's drawing pictured on page 16. If your child's picture has a number of different elements, such as a house and a car and a person, you can make toys out of all of them!

What you need

- 50 cm (20 in) square of white cotton fabric for the front
- 50 cm (20 in) square of cotton or minky fabric for the back
- polyester stuffing
- iron-on transfer paper
- computer and ink-jet printer
- basic sewing kit (page 65)

What to do

1. Open the digital copy of your child's artwork in a picture-editing program on your computer, such as Photoshop, Paint or Picnik. Flip the image on the horizontal axis (otherwise it will be back-to-front when you do your transfer). You might also want to adjust the contrast or make the colours brighter if necessary.

2. Print the flipped image onto the transfer paper following the instructions on the packet.

3. Trim the transfer paper, cutting closely around the edges of the image, then iron it onto the white cotton following the manufacturer's instructions.

4. If you're making multiple toys, you can iron all of the artworks onto one big piece of fabric – just remember to leave a 4 cm (1½ in) space between each image for cutting out and seam allowance.

5. Once you have transferred your image to the fabric, cut around the picture, leaving space for a border (if you wish) and a 5 mm (¼ in) seam allowance. Pin the shape to the backing fabric with right sides together, then cut to the shape of the front piece.

6. Sew all the way around the edges of the shape using a 5 mm seam allowance and leaving a 5 cm (2 in) opening. Turn right way out (you can use a knitting needle to poke out any tricky bits) and press flat with an iron.
7. Push the polyester stuffing in through the opening. The trick with stuffing is to use a little at a time, packing it nice and firm (but not so firm that your seams rip open).
8. Now sew the opening closed using a ladder stitch (see page 72).

tips + tricks

There are many different brands of transfer paper to choose from and some of them have different effects – it's trial and error until you discover the brand you like best.

Inspired by American designers Ray and Charles Eames, this project can be made as an interesting and challenging puzzle, or just as pretty cards for your child to interlock like clever building blocks.

What you need

- traced Puzzle template (page 219)
- sheets of thin, stiff cardboard to match the size of the artworks
- scissors or craft knife
- paper paste, PVA glue, spray adhesive or glue stick
- sharp, light pencil

What to do

1. Cut out Puzzle template carefully using sharp scissors or a craft knife.
2. Glue your artworks to both sides of the cardboard – make sure you have a complete coverage of glue, or else the paper will peel off. You can use paper paste or PVA glue (thinned with a little water) applied with a paintbrush, spray adhesive, or a glue stick. Smooth out any air bubbles as you go, and leave to dry.
3. Trace the template onto the glued artworks with a pencil. Trace each shape beside the previous one so that the pictures line up when the puzzle is assembled. You want to have at least eight puzzle pieces, but you can make as many as you want.
4. Cut out the puzzle pieces carefully using sharp scissors or a craft knife.

tips + tricks

You can use this technique to make cards for a game of snap. Glue your artworks to one side of the cardboard only (leaving the other side blank) and cut just two cards from each artwork, or make sure you have pairs that match in colour.

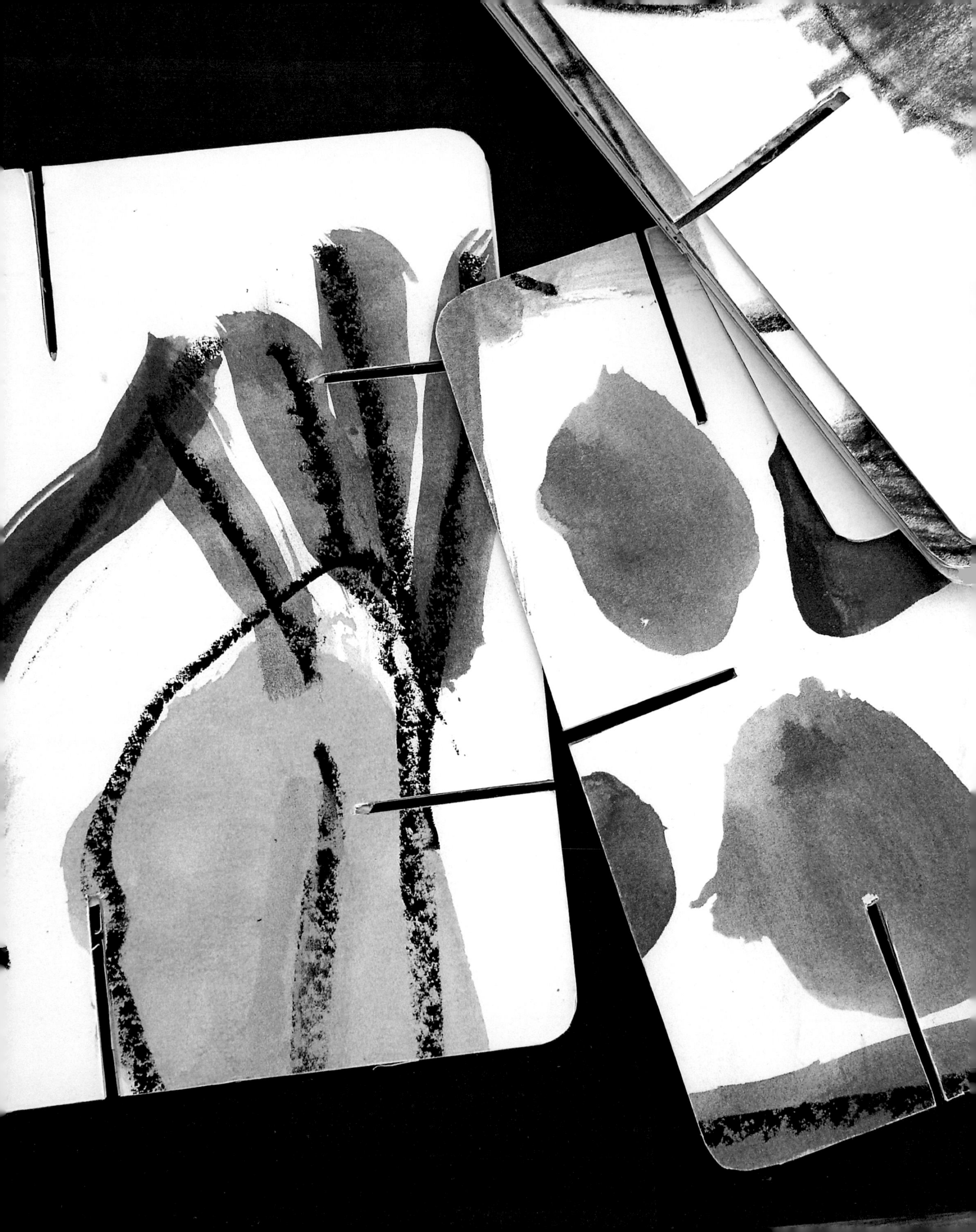

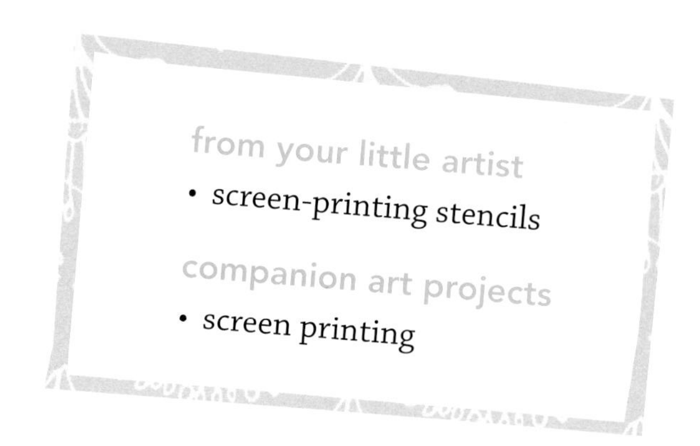

This gorgeous mobile is great for adding some colour to a bedroom. When hung above a cot, this is a lovely way for little artists to share their work with a new sibling.

What you need

- tissue paper in a variety of colours
- laminator and laminating pouches
- permanent marker
- galvanised wire
- fishing line
- scissors
- hole punch
- pliers

What to do

1. Cut or tear the tissue paper into various shapes, such as strips, circles and squares. Arrange the shapes inside the laminating pouch and then feed through the laminator. Make sure you leave some little gaps between the tissue-paper pieces, as this helps the laminate hold together. (If you don't have access to a laminator, you can use clear contact paper. However, the shapes can end up a bit floppy, so this only works with small designs.)

2. Using a permanent marker, trace the stencils onto the laminated sheet, then cut out the shapes with the scissors. You will need at least eight pieces.

3. Punch a small hole in the centre-top of each shape and then tie a piece of fishing line, about 30 cm (12 in) long, through each of the holes.

4. Cut two pieces of wire about 30 cm (12 in) long. Using the pliers, bend and twist one of the pieces of wire to make a loop in the centre. Thread the second piece of wire through the loop, then bend the wire down and make a twist so that the two wires are interlocked. Curl the ends of each piece of wire upwards to make little loops. Tie a piece of fishing line, about 80 cm (31½ in) long, through the centre loop.

5 Cut four pieces of wire about 15 cm (6 in) long. Using the pliers, bend a loop in the centre of each piece and curl the ends in. Tie pieces of fishing line, about 30 cm (12 in) long, through each of the centre loops.

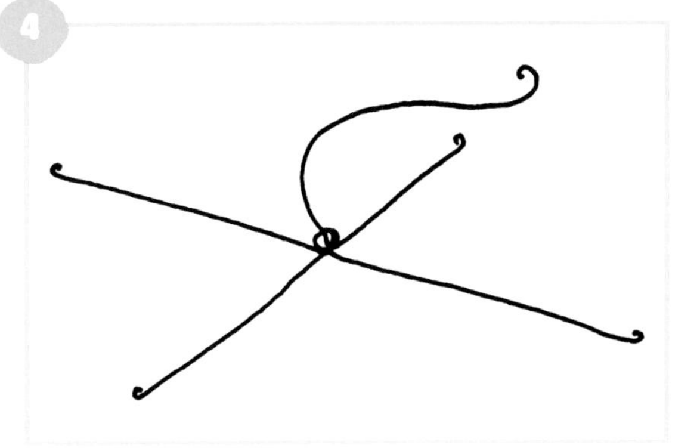

6 Tie the line attached to each short piece of wire to each of the ends of the cross-piece, allowing them to hang at varying heights. Then tie each of your laminated shapes to the ends of the short pieces. This is the most fun (and challenging!) part of making a mobile, as you have to play around with the hanging lengths of your pieces in order to make everything balance – it's much easier if you hang your mobile up to do this.

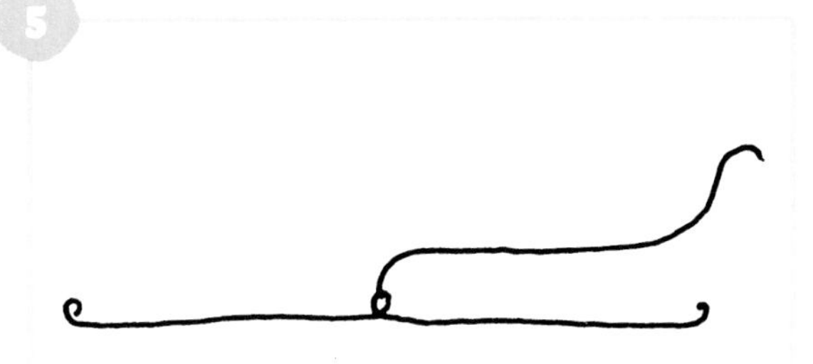

tips + tricks

This mobile will look beautiful hanging next to the matching screen print framed on a wall or printed onto a table runner or cushion. Repeating design elements throughout the home creates a sense of continuity and familiarity which in turn brings warmth to the space.

from your little artist

- art for making a digital copy (see page 63)

companion art projects

- any art project

STICKERS

Making stickers from scratch is a wonderful rainy day activity. Keep the finished stickers together in a little box or stick them to a postcard, birthday parcel or lunch wrapper. These homemade stickers make a lovely gift when paired with the letter set on page 199.

What you need

- 1 tablespoon water
- ¼ tablespoon vinegar
- 2 tablespoons non-toxic craft glue
- scissors
- bowl
- paintbrush

What to do

1. Photocopy or print your child's artwork (you may need to shrink the images to make them a good size for stickers). Print as many pictures as you can on each piece of paper, to avoid waste.

2. Cut your pictures out with scissors. I like to leave a 1–2 mm (⅛ in) border of white around the pictures.

3. In a small bowl, mix the water, vinegar and craft glue until smooth. This sticker glue will keep in an air-tight jar for up to a week.

4. Brush a thin layer of the glue onto the back of each shape, then leave to dry. The stickers will probably curl up a bit – if so, once the glue is completely dry, pop them in a heavy book for a few days to flatten them out before use.

5. To use the stickers, dab the glue side onto a wet sponge (or you can use a paintbrush to brush with a little water). Try using your stickers to seal an envelope containing a message of love or thanks. Who doesn't love receiving mail, especially when it has stickers?

tips + tricks

If you have one, you can use a sticker-making machine to make your stickers. (You may need to resize the drawings to make them small enough to fit through the machine.) Just print out your images, cut the paper into strips, line them up on the tray and you can crank out metres of stickers!

You can buy many different brands of sticker-making machines, such as Xyron and Esselte, from sewing and craft-supply shops. Always read the manufacturer's instructions before use.

LILY
IF YOU SEEK
SHELTER, LOOK FOR
A BIG ELEPHANT.
You are good shelter!

The key to this project is choosing a stencil that suits. For the bookmark, the stencil shape should be a creature with at least two legs at the bottom so that a page may be slipped between them; for the bag tag, there should be a spot where the tag extension can be added – Lily's dinosaur print on page 46 was ideal.

What you need

- Bag-tag template (page 224)
- sheets of polypropylene
- cutting mat
- soft pencil or permanent marker
- sharp scissors or craft knife

What to do

Once you have chosen your stencils to use, check that they are at a size that makes sense for a book or tag – not too big (over 15 cm/6 in wide) and not too small (under 5 cm/2 in wide). You can resize the stencil design on the photocopier if you need.

Lay a sheet of polypropylene on the cutting mat. (You may like to cut the sheet to a more manageable size first.) Place the stencil on top and, if you are making the bag tag, place the template at the top of the stencil as an extension. Trace around the stencil using a soft pencil or permanent marker.

Cut the design out of the polypropylene using small sharp scissors. You can rub out any stray pencil marks with an eraser. If there are fiddly bits in the design which you can't get to with scissors, you will need to use a craft knife. Don't try to cut the plastic in one go and remember to keep your fingers and hands away from the front of the blade when cutting, as the blade can slip on the plastic.

If you are making the bag tag, cut a 2.5 cm (1 in) horizontal line into the design, 2 cm (¾ in) from the top edge, so that the tag can be bent around and fastened.

tips + tricks
These cute little critters also look lovely hanging in the Lullaby Mobile (page 85).

from your little artist

- art for tracing

companion art projects

- any art project

EMBROIDERED TOY

Choose a piece of your child's artwork that depicts something suitable for a toy (and isn't too complicated), such as a person or animal. When Lily made the gorgeous lino print pictured on page 42, I just couldnt wait to make a toy from her design.

What you need

- 70 cm (27½ in) square of plain cotton fabric
- felt and fabric for appliqué
- polyester stuffing
- embroidery hoop (optional)
- transfer pencil
- tracing paper
- knitting needle (optional)
- basic sewing kit (page 65)

What to do

1. Cut the plain cotton fabric in half so you have two rectangles.
2. Trace your child's artwork onto tracing paper using a transfer pencil. Iron the transfer onto the right side of one of the pieces of fabric, following the manufacturer's instructions – this provides a guide for your appliqué and embroidery.
3. Cut out the appliqué shapes you've drawn on the tracing paper, pin them to the felt or fabric, and cut. Pin the shapes to the front fabric piece, using the transfer lines as a guide, and stitch on using a sewing machine or needle and thread. Stretch the fabric in an embroidery hoop if you are hand stitching – you can use straight stitch, back stitch or blanket stitch (see pages 72–3).
4. Embroider over any remaining transfer lines using back stitch or straight stitch or you can use a sewing machine.

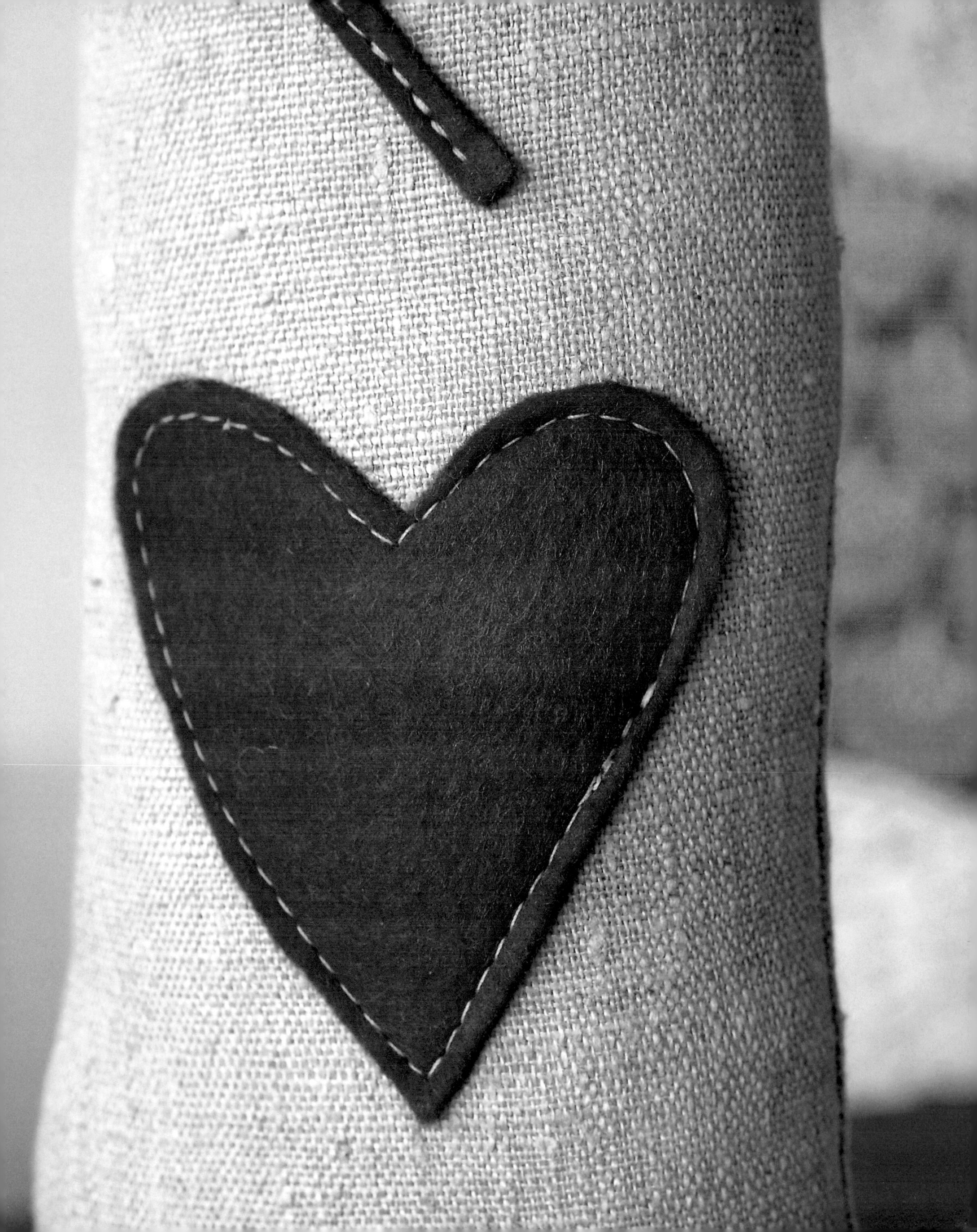

What to do

1. Pin the embroidered fabric to the plain piece of fabric with wrong sides facing. Cut the fabric into the shape you want your toy to be, making sure you leave a 5 mm (¼ in) seam allowance around the edges. Now pin the fabric together with right sides facing and stitch all the way around the edges leaving a 5 cm (2 in) opening for stuffing. (Don't position the opening too close to an arm or leg, if your design has them, otherwise the final stitching can get tricky.) Identify any weak points where stitching might come undone (such as where arms and legs join the body) and stitch over the seam a few times.

2. Make a few little snips into any corners and curves so that they don't bunch up when turned right-side out (be careful not to cut through the stitching).

3. Turn the toy right way out – you may need to use a knitting needle to poke out any tricky corners. Gently rub any stubborn edges between thumb and forefinger until they are eased out. Press with an iron.

4. Push the polyester stuffing in through the opening. The trick with stuffing is to use a little at a time, packing it nice and firm (but not so firm that your seams rip open).

5. Now close up the stuffing opening using a ladder stitch (page 72) and you're done!

tips + tricks

I like to call these kinds of toys 'flats', since you start with a 2D shape. The stuffing gives the shape enough dimension and depth for it to become a beloved toy. After a bit of practice making 'flats' you might like to incorporate some tried and tested 3D toy-making techniques found in books such as *Softies* and *More Softies*.

from your little artist

- printed fabric

companion art projects

- faux lino-printing
- screen printing
- Gocco printing

CUDDLE QUILT

Before I made this quilt, I'd been keeping all of Lily's wonderful prints in a drawer where no one could see them. What was I thinking? This is a nice simple patchwork and is a great introduction to quilting. You can use the same method to create a much larger quilt – just add more squares!

What you need

- fabric pieces in complementary patterns and colours to sew into a 50 cm (20 in) square for the front
- 24 cm × 60 cm (9½ in × 24 in) plain fabric for the front border
- 60 cm (24 in) square of soft fabric for the back
- 50 cm (20 in) square of quilt batting
- basic sewing kit (page 65)

What to do

Cut the front fabric pieces into 49 squares, each 8 cm × 8 cm (3 in × 3 in). Arrange the squares in a 7 × 7 grid, swapping them around until you're happy with the arrangement of patterns and colours. Gather the pieces up in rows, making seven piles of seven squares.

Take the top two squares from your first pile and place them together with right sides facing. Stitch along one edge with your sewing machine, leaving a 5 mm seam allowance. Unfold the squares, place the third square on top of the second square with right sides facing and stitch along the edge opposite the seam. Repeat until you have sewn the seven squares into a strip. Press seams flat with an iron.

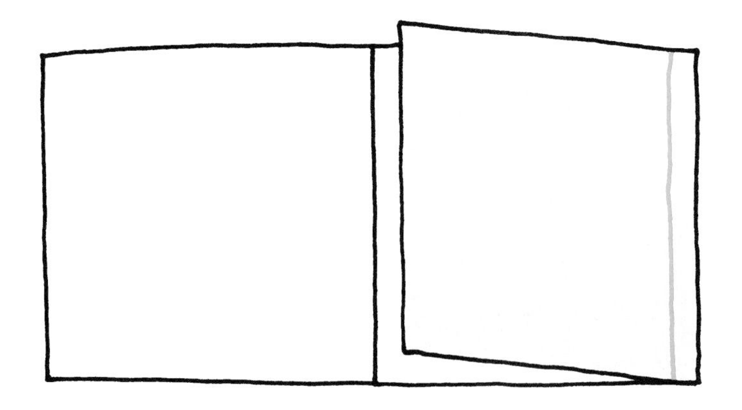

3. Repeat step 2 with each pile of fabric, until you have seven strips. Lay the strips out in your original grid arrangement.

4. Take the top-row strip and the second-row strip and place them together with right sides facing. Make sure the strips are placed together the right way round (I find it helps to take note of the pattern or colour of the left-hand square on each row, and then you just have to make sure they are placed on top of each other). Stitch together along the bottom edge of the top row, leaving a 5mm (¼ in) seam allowance.

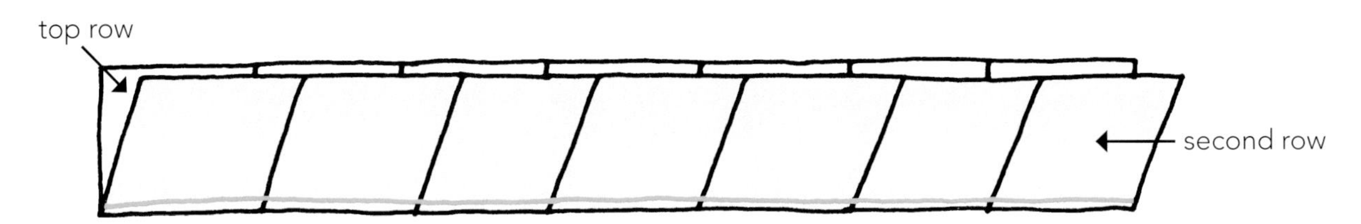

5. Place the third-row strip on top of the second row strip with right sides facing, and stitch together along the bottom edge of the second row. Repeat until you have sewn all of the strips together into a square. Press the seams flat with an iron.

6. Cut the front-border fabric into two 6 cm × 60 cm (2¼ in × 24 in) strips and two 6 cm × 50 cm (2¼ in × 20 in) strips. Pin the shorter strips to opposite edges of the patchwork with right sides facing. Sew together leaving a 5 mm (¼ in) seam allowance, then sew the longer strips to the remaining edges. Press the seams flat with an iron.

7. Place the patchwork front piece on the batting, right side facing up, then place the back piece on top, right side down. Pin together, placing some pins around the middle as well, so that the batting is nice and secure.

8. Sew all the way around the edges, leaving a 1 cm (⅜ in) seam allowance and a 5 cm (2 in) opening on one side for turning right way out. Be sure to back-stitch at the beginning and end so that the stitching doesn't come undone.

9. Turn right side out and press flat with an iron. Starting in a corner, top-stitch all the way around the cuddle quilt, 2–3 mm (⅛ in) from the edge (this will stitch the opening closed).

What to do

Starting at the bottom left-hand corner of the top left-hand square, topstitch a diagonal line at 45 degrees across the square. When you get to the corner, with the sewing-machine needle down, lift the foot and turn the quilt so that you can keep sewing along the top of the next square. Lower the foot and stitch along until you get to the next corner, then lift the foot again, turn the quilt and stitch diagonally across the two squares, parallel to your first row of stitching (as shown in the first picture below). Continue in this way until there are diagonal lines running through all of the squares (as shown in the second picture below).

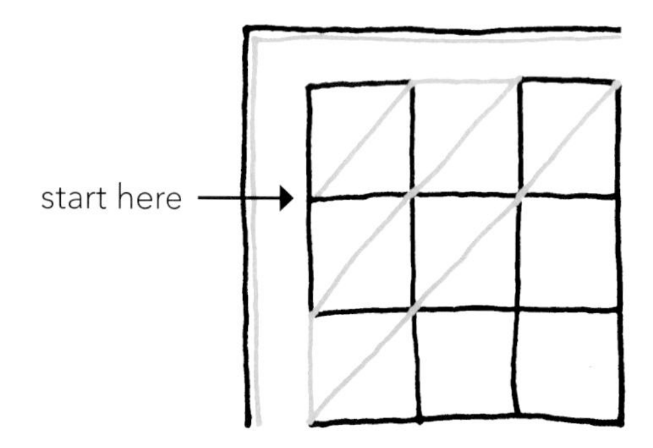

Now topstitch diagonally across all of the squares in the other direction, starting at the bottom right-hand corner of the top right-hand square.

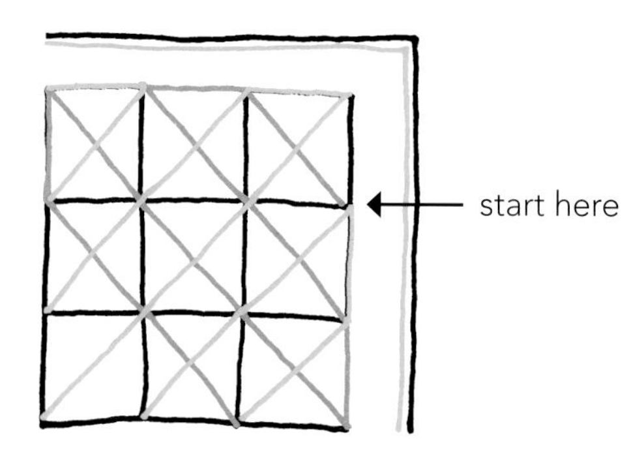

Trim off the threads and you're done. Time to cuddle!

tips + tricks

I love using really soft minky or polar fleece for the backing fabric to make this quilt extra cuddly.

TO WEAR

ART SMOCK

I love making art smocks out of fabric from less-successful printing days. It's a great way to avoid waste and if the prints are a little smudgy it doesn't matter – they will soon be covered in colourful layers of paint and ink (and maybe a little bit of cake).

What you need

- Art Smock template (page 220)
- 50 cm (20 in) square printed fabric for the outer
- 50 cm (20 in) square plain fabric for the lining
- basic sewing kit (page 65)

What to do

1. Photocopy and cut out the Art Smock template. Fold your printed fabric in half and pin on the template piece. Cut, then do the same with the plain fabric (or you can lay one folded fabric piece on top of the other and cut both at once.
2. Pin the front and back pieces together with right sides facing.
3. Beginning at one end of the opening, as marked on the template, sew the front and back pieces together, leaving a 5 mm (¼ in) seam allowance. Stitch all the way around the edge, leaving the opening so that you can turn the smock right way out. Be sure to back-stitch at the beginning and end so that the stitching doesn't come undone.
4. Turn the smock right side out through the opening and iron flat. Hand-sew the opening shut using a ladder stitch (page 72).
5. Cross the shoulder-back pieces over each other so that they meet the opposite shoulder-front edges. Make sure nothing is twisted, then overlap the edges slightly and pin together. Stitch in place with your sewing machine.
6. Now pop over your little one's head and get painting!

tips + tricks

For the lining fabric, cut up an old shirt or bed sheet.

from your little artist

- printed fabric

companion art projects

- faux lino printing
- screen printing
- gocco printing

FRENCHY SCARF

What I love most about this scarf (in addition to how adorable it looks) is that young children, who have a tendency to misplace things, cannot possibly drop this as it is secured gently by a loop.

What you need

- traced Frenchy Scarf template (page 222)
- 15 cm × 80 cm (6 in × 31½ in) printed fabric for the front
- 15 cm × 80 cm (6 in × 31½ in) plain fabric for the back
- basic sewing kit (page 65)

What to do

1. Cut out the Frenchy Scarf template. Fold your printed fabric in half so that the short edges are together, and pin on the template piece. Cut, then do the same with the plain fabric (or you can lay one folded fabric piece on top of the other and cut both at once).

2. Unfold the fabric, and, with tailor's chalk, mark the dots from the pattern piece onto one end of one of your fabric pieces (on the wrong side of the fabric). Pin the front and back pieces together with right sides facing.

3. Starting at one of the marked opening dots, sew all the way around the edge of the scarf, leaving a 5 mm (¼ in) seam allowance, until you get to the next mark. Be sure to back-stitch at the beginning and end so that the stitching doesn't come undone.

4. Continue sewing around the edge between the remaining two dots. You should now have two openings directly opposite each other in the sides of the scarf. This is the hole you will use to thread one end of the scarf through the other in order to secure it around your little one's neck.

tips + tricks

You can make an adult-sized scarf with this pattern – just enlarge the template by 400%.

5 Turn the scarf right way out through one of the openings and iron flat. Neaten by topstitching 3 mm (⅛ in) from the edge all the way around the scarf, starting and stopping on either side of each opening.

With a dye bath and a Gocco screen, you can make a plain singlet into something really special. You can adapt this project to use with any piece of clothing – a t-shirt, shorts or a dress – whatever you have that needs a bit of sprucing up!

What you need

- white cotton singlet
- fabric dye
- bucket
- materials for Gocco printing (page 54)
- scrap paper or newspaper
- iron

What to do

Fill up a bucket with hot water and prepare the dye bath as per the instructions on the packet. Wet the singlet with hot water and then add to the dye bath. Stir the garment around in the dye for 10–30 minutes, depending on how dark you want the colour to be.

Rinse the singlet in warm water until the water runs clear. Wash with clean warm water and a small amount of detergent and then rinse thoroughly in cold water. Hang up to air dry.

Iron the singlet once it's dry, then lay it out on a flat surface with the front facing up. Insert some scrap paper or newspaper into the singlet in order to prevent the back from absorbing any ink.

Lay the Gocco screen on top of the singlet. Plop a generous amount of ink across the top of the screen and drag the squeegee firmly over the screen towards you (for more detailed instructions, see page 54).

Gently peel the screen off the fabric (you may need to hold the singlet down so that it doesn't shift and smudge). Allow to dry as per the ink instructions, then iron on a high setting for 5 minutes to set the ink.

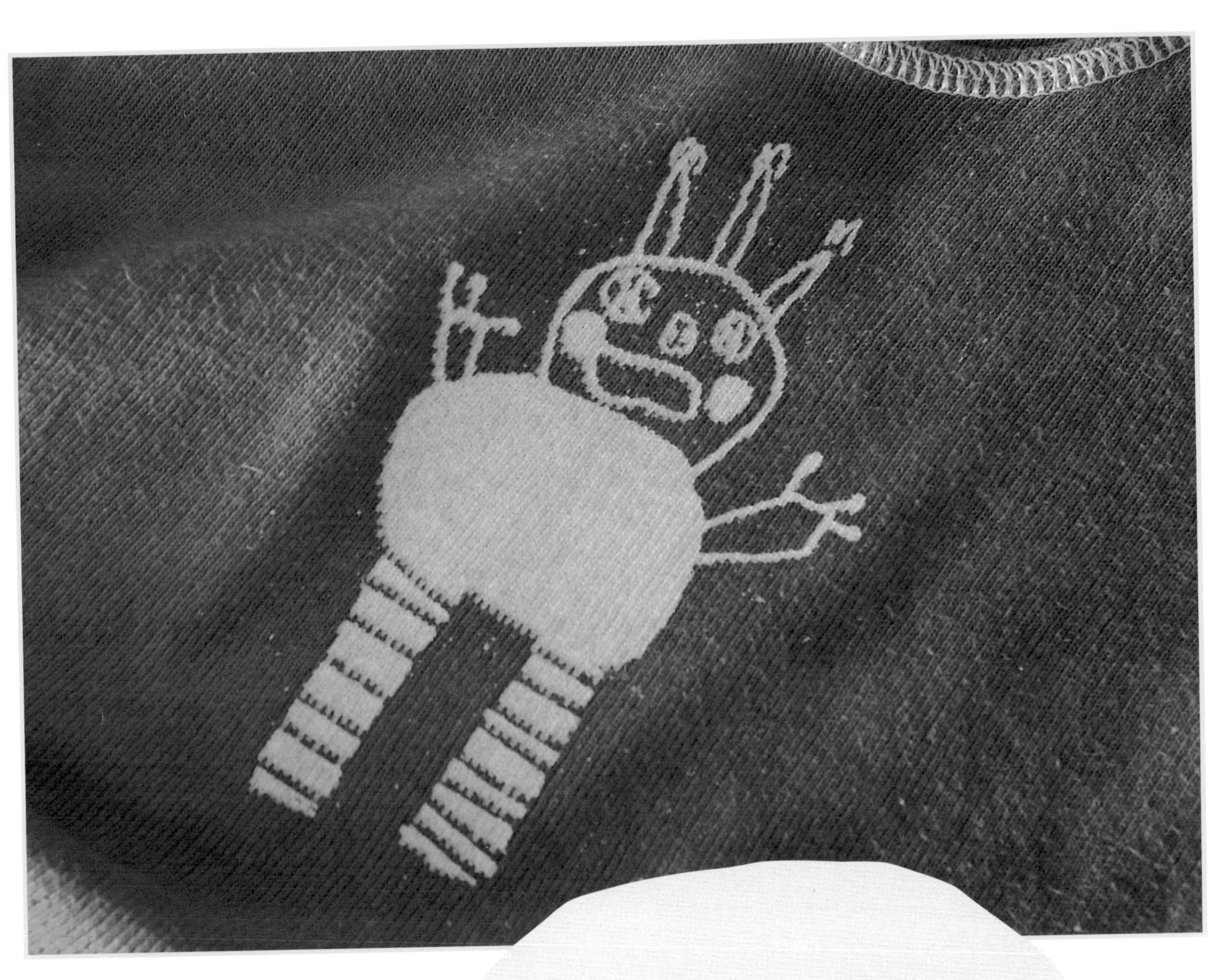

tips + tricks

Fabric dye is a fun and cheap way to give boring old clothes a new life. You don't have to just go for a solid colour effect, either – try bunching the fabric up with rubber bands for a great tie-dye look, or dipping only one half of the garment in the dye for a striking ombré effect.

from your little artist

- art for tracing

companion art projects

- any art project

FOLK HANDBAG

Why spend money on an expensive handbag when it's so simple to make your own? The bold shapes of Lily's flowers in her drawing on page 20 made a striking decoration and were remarkable easy to appliqué.

What you need

- Folk Handbag template (page 225)
- 50 cm × 100 cm (20 in × 40 in) plain heavy fabric such as wool, felt or blanketing for the outer bag
- 50 cm × 100 cm (20 in × 40 in) patterned cotton fabric for the lining
- 50 cm × 100 cm (20 in × 40 in) iron-on fusible interfacing
- wool felt
- bag handles
- tracing paper
- pencil
- basic sewing kit (page 65)

What to do

Trace your child's artwork onto tracing paper, then cut out to use as a template. Pin the tracing paper pieces to the felt and cut out the shapes.

Photocopy and cut out the Folk Handbag template. Iron the interfacing to the lining fabric (this will help the bag keep its shape). Place the outer fabric and lining fabric together with right sides facing, pin the template pieces and cut out the bag pieces following the instructions on the template. You will have five outer fabric pieces and three lining pieces.

Pin your felt shapes to the right side of one (or both) of the Side A pieces cut from the outer fabric. Appliqué the felt shapes with your sewing machine, or by hand using straight stitch, back stitch or blanket stitch (see pages 72–3).

Fold each handle-loop piece in half with right-sides together, as indicated on the template. Stitch up the short sides, turn the right way out and press.

What to do *continued*

With right sides together, sew the Side A lining pieces to the Side B lining piece. Side B will make the narrow sides and the base of your bag, leaving the straight edge at the top as the bag opening.

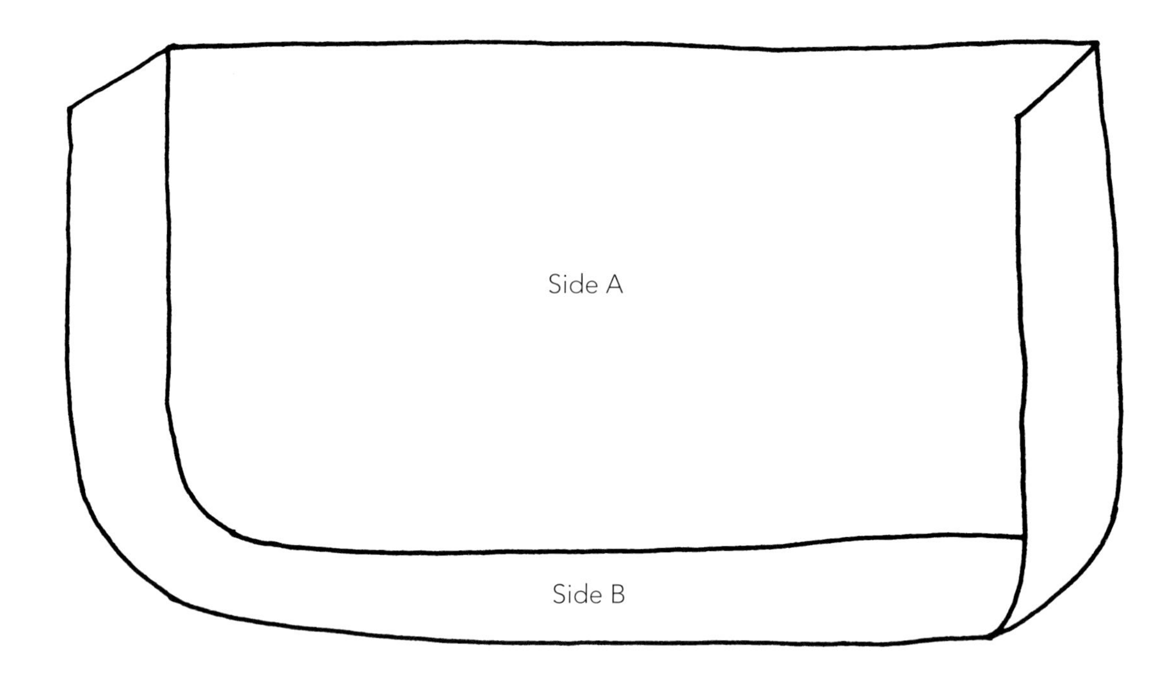

Do the same with the outer fabric (you will end up with what looks like two bags).

Turn the lining right way out, and insert into the outer bag, so that right sides are together and seams are matched up (it should look like an inside-out bag).

Sandwich your handle-loop pieces between the outer bag and the lining with the raw edges together. Make sure the loop handles are in the centre of the top edge of the bag and line up on both sides. Pin into place.

Sew around the top edge of the bag, leaving a 5 cm (2 in) opening for turning the right way out, securing the handle loops in place as you go.

10 Turn the right way out, push the lining down inside the outer bag, and iron flat. Sew the opening closed using a ladder stitch (page 72).

11 The handle loop tabs should now be sticking out of the top edge of your bag. Thread the loop tab through the slot in the handle (or just over the bottom of the handle, if it doesn't have a slot). Fold the tab over towards the inside of the bag so that the handle is nice and tight against the top edge of the bag. Pin into place. (Depending on how thick your handles are, the tab might still be quite long – you can fold the end of the tab underneath before pinning to make it shorter.) Stitch the tab down nice and close to the top edge of the bag. (It's a good idea to go over this twice to make sure the handles are firmly in place.)

tips + tricks

This pattern can be easily adapted to suit your needs. Try enlarging the template even more to make a shopping tote, or less for an evening bag!

I used some leaves from the background Lily's drawing on page 18 as inspiration for these lovely brooches. You can make them out of polymer clay or felt.

What you need

- wool felt
- polymer clay such as Fimo or Sculpey
- brooch backs
- needle and embroidery threads
- tracing paper
- pencil
- scissors
- superglue
- craft knife (optional)
- sewing machine (optional)

What to do

Felt brooch

1. Trace your child's artwork onto tracing paper using a pencil, then cut out the shapes to use as templates. It's best to use a piece of art that features big bold shapes without too much detail.

2. Pin the baking-paper pieces to the felt and cut out the shapes. For each brooch, cut two of the same shape in different colours, then trim the edge of the piece you'd like on top by 1–2 mm (⅛ in) all the way around.

3. Stitch the two pieces together (you can do this with a sewing machine or by hand). Use thread in a contrasting colour if you'd like to embroider some detail onto the brooch.

4. Hand-stitch your brooch back to the middle of the larger piece of felt. Go over the stitching a few times so that it doesn't become loose, as you would if you were sewing on a button.

Clay brooch

1. You can roll out the polymer clay to a thickness of 5 mm (¼ in) and cut around a stencil (as in the felt brooch instructions) with a craft knife, or you can sculpt your shape just using your child's art as a guide.

2. Bake the clay in your oven, following the manufacturer's instructions.

3. Attach the brooch back to the clay using superglue (check the manufacturer's instructions before use). Resist the urge to wear your lovely brooch straight away – leaving the glue to set for 24 hours will give the best results.

tips + tricks

You can easily add more decoration to your brooches – try sewing buttons, ribbon, sequins, beads or googly eyes onto a felt brooch, or attaching decorations to a clay brooch with superglue.

from your little artist

- a screen-printing stencil or Gocco-screen

companion art projects

- screen printing
- Gocco printing

LIBRARY BAG

The perfect accessory for a trip to the library. Your little one will be itching to fill this bag with wonderful books!

What you need

- plain calico bag
- scrap paper or newspaper
- materials for screen printing (page 48) or Gocco printing (page 54)
- iron

What to do

1. Wash and dry your calico bag, then iron it nice and flat. Insert some scrap paper or newspaper into the bag in order to prevent the back panel from absorbing any ink.

2. Lay the stencil down in the desired position (skip this if you are using a Gocco screen) and place the screen on top. Plop a generous amount of ink across the top of the screen and drag the squeegee firmly over the screen towards you (for more detailed instructions, see page 48 or 54).

3. Gently peel the screen off the fabric (you may need to hold the bag down flat so that it doesn't shift and smudge). Allow to dry as per the ink instructions, then iron on a high setting for 5 minutes to set the ink.

from your little artist

- printed fabric

companion art projects

- faux lino printing
- screen printing
- Gocco printing

SUNNY HAT

Kids won't need any convincing to slap on this funky hat before going out to play in the sun. Who wouldn't want to show off a hat printed with their own amazing art?

What you need

- Sunny Hat template (page 226)
- 50 cm (20 in) square of printed fabric for the outer
- 50 cm (20 in) square of plain fabric for the lining
- 2 metres (2 yd) of 5 mm (¼ in) gauge wire
- basic sewing kit (page 65)

What to do

Photocopy and cut out the Sunny Hat template. Fold your printed fabric in half and pin on the template pieces, matching the fold lines marked on the template with the folded edge of the fabric. Cut out the pieces. Repeat with the plain fabric (or you can lay one folded fabric piece on top of the other and cut both at the same time).

(Note: Follow steps 2–5 with the printed outer fabric and then with the plain lining fabric – you will essentially make two hats.) With right sides facing, sew the short ends of the crown piece together, leaving a 1 cm (⅜ in) seam allowance, to form a loop.

This is the trickiest part: pin the crown piece around the edge of the circular top piece with right sides facing and stitch together leaving a 1 cm (⅜ in) seam allowance. (If you get muddled here, don't worry – I often end up having to unpick and resew my top piece in order for it to sit straight.)

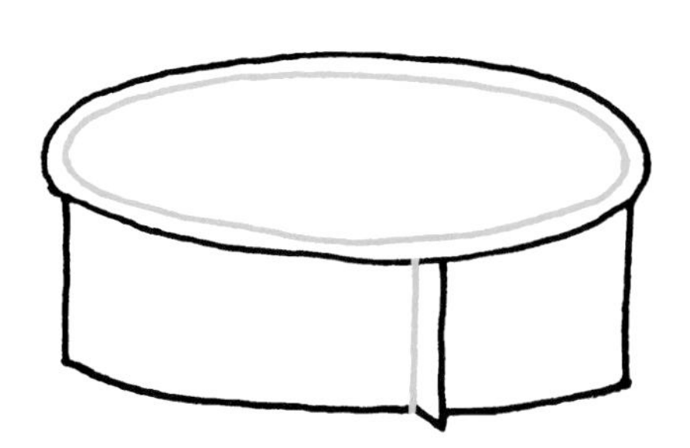

tips + tricks

If you don't want to use wire in the brim, you can use iron-on interfacing. Cut out the interfacing using the brim template piece and iron onto the wrong side of your lining fabric with a warm iron for 3–5 minutes. Follow the sewing instructions given, just skip step 7. You can make the brim extra stiff by sewing additional rows of topstitching around the edge of the brim, spaced 1–2 cm (3⁄8–3⁄4 in) apart.

What to do *continued*

4. With right sides facing, sew the two brim pieces together along the short edges leaving a 1 cm (⅜ in) seam allowance. Once sewn together, your brim pieces should form a doughnut shape.

5. Now pin the raw edge of the crown piece to the inside edge of the brim with right sides facing. Match up the seam in the crown piece with one of the seams on the brim. Stitch together leaving a 1 cm (⅜ in) seam allowance.

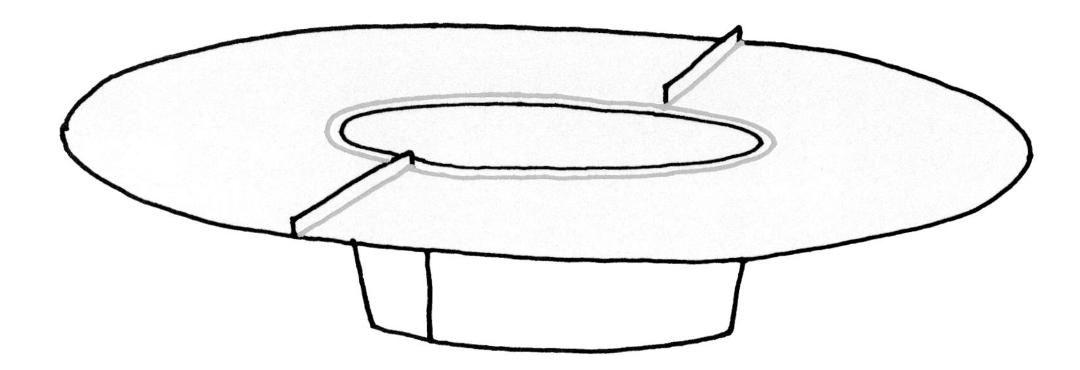

6. You should now have an outer-fabric hat and a lining hat. Turn one hat right side out and place over the other hat, so right sides are facing and the raw edges of the brims are together. Sew all the way around the edge of the brim using a 1 cm (⅜ in) seam allowance, leaving a 5 cm (2 in) opening for turning right side out. Turn the hat right way out and iron seams flat.

7. Bend the piece of wire into a circle the same size as the edge of the brim, leaving a little bit of an overlap at the ends (it helps if the wire circle is a tiny bit bigger than the brim, as the tension will hold the brim out nicely). Trim the wire if necessary. Push the wire in through the opening in the brim so that it sits inside the edge of the brim. Twist the ends of the wire together to keep it in place.

8. Sew the opening closed using a ladder stitch (see page 72).Topstitch all the way around the brim, with your presser foot right alongside the inside edge of the wire. Finally, topstitch around the brim near where it meets the crown (this just helps the two sides of your hat sit together nicely). Now pop the hat on your little one's head and take them out to play in the sunshine!

FOR HOME

from your little artist

- printed fabric

companion art projects

- faux lino printing
- screen printing
- Gocco printing

PATCHWORK CUSHION

You can use fabric with any colours and patterns you like for this project; I like to cut the strips from a combination of hand-printed fabric, solid-colour fabric and complementary patterned fabric.

What you need

- Patchwork Cushion template (page 228)
- fabric pieces in complementary patterns and colours to sew into a 42 cm (16½ in) square for the front
- 42 cm × 32 cm (16½ in × 12½ in) plain cotton fabric for the back
- 42 cm × 22 cm (16½ in × 8½ in) plain cotton fabric for the back
- 42 cm (16½ in) square piece of quilt batting
- 40 cm (16 in) square cushion insert
- basic sewing kit (page 65)

What to do

1. Photocopy and cut out the Patchwork Cushion template, pin the pieces to your fabric scraps (make sure the straight edges of the rectangles run parallel with the grain of the fabric) and cut them out.

2. Using the diagram opposite as a guide, make your patchwork. Always place right sides together and leave a 5 mm (¼ in) seam allowance. It is also really helpful to iron the seams flat as you go. Start by sewing piece 1 to piece 2, then sew piece 3 to those joined pieces, then piece 4, and so on, until you have sewn all of the rectangles together into a 42 cm (16½ in) square.

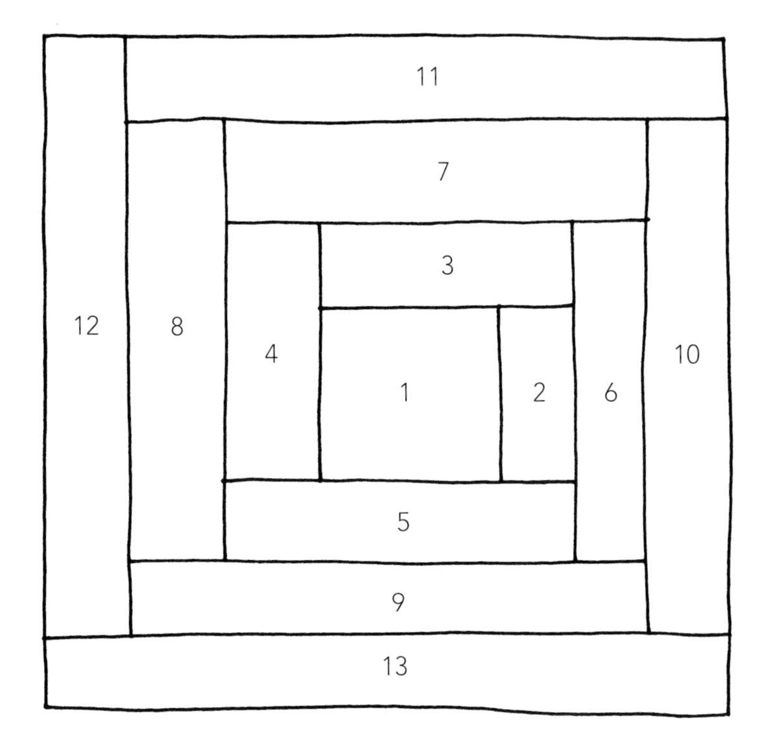

Lay the batting out and place your patchwork on top, right side facing up. Pin together, placing some pins around the middle as well, so that the batting is nice and secure. Using your sewing machine, topstitch a square which runs through the centre of pieces 2, 3, 4 and 5, as shown. Then sew a square which runs through pieces 6, 7, 8 and 9, and a third square through pieces 10, 11, 12 and 13.

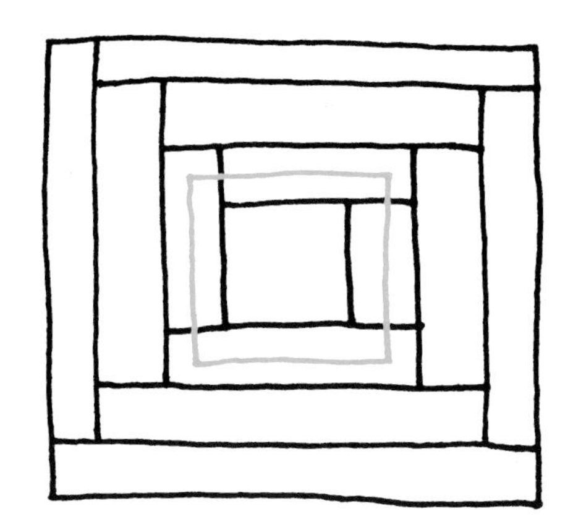

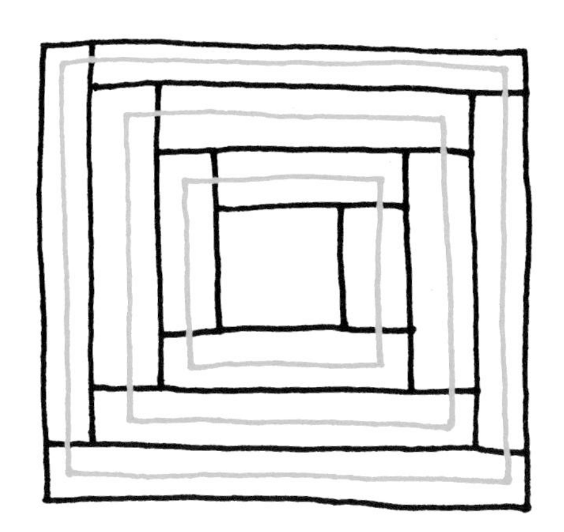

What to do continued

4. For the back of your cushion cover, take the two plain fabric rectangles and hem one long edge on each. To create a hem, fold the edge over (wrong sides together) by 1 cm (3/8 in). Press with an iron, fold over another 1 cm (3/8 in), press again and then stitch down with your sewing machine.

5. Place the larger back piece on top of the quilted top piece with raw edges together and right sides facing. Place the smaller piece on top, lining up the raw edges so that the hemmed edges overlap. Pin into place, then stitch all the way around with your sewing machine, leaving a 1.5 cm (5/8 in) seam allowance.

6. Neaten the raw edges with an overlocker or zigzag stitch on your sewing machine. Turn your cover right way out, and stuff in the insert. Now curl up on the couch with your cushion and a good book.

tips + tricks
The finished cover will actually be a little smaller than the insert – this way the cushion turns out nice and plump!

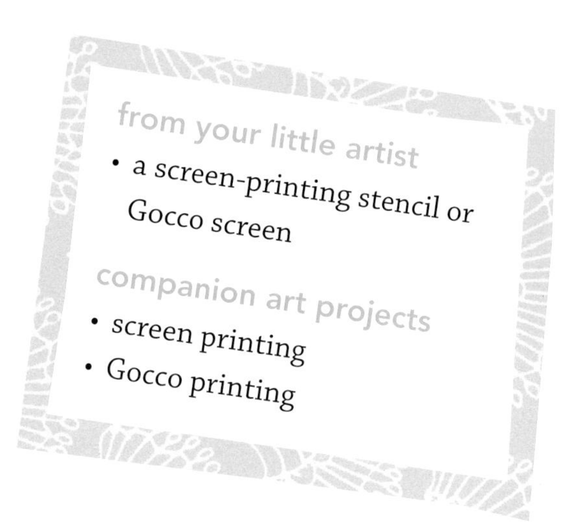

PRINTED STOOL

Turn an old piece of furniture – or even a new one – into a work of art with this simple project. Try printing a set of stools in different colours using the one stencil – or in one colour using different stencils – you'll be amazed at the results!

What you need

- unvarnished wooden stool (or other furniture)
- sandpaper (optional)
- materials for screen printing (page 48) or Gocco printing (page 54)
- furniture varnish

What to do

Give the stool a wipe with a dry cloth to remove any dust. If the piece you are using does have paint or varnish on it, you can sand it back and then wipe it down to make sure the wood is clean and dust free.

Lay the stencil down in the desired position (skip this if you are using a Gocco screen) and place the screen on top. Plop a generous amount of ink across the top of the screen and drag the squeegee firmly over the screen towards you (for more detailed instructions, see page 48 or 54).

Gently peel the screen off the printed surface (you may need to hold onto the stool so that it doesn't shift and smudge the ink). Allow to dry as per the ink instructions.

If printing numerous images onto the stool, leave your first print to dry before printing again so that your images don't get smudged (remember to wash out your screen between uses so that the ink doesn't dry and clog it up).

Once all your layers are dry (leave 24 hours to be sure) you can gently brush on or spray on a coat of varnish following the manufacturer's instructions.

PACIFIC OCEAN
SOUTH AMERICA
ARGENTINA
URUGUAY
BOLIVIA
BRAZIL
COLOMBIA
VENEZUELA
UNITED STATES
ONTARIO
QUEBEC
LABRADOR
NEWFOUNDLAND
NORTH
KING FREDERIK VI LAND
ICELAND
Reykjavik
GREAT BRITAIN
IRELAND
N.IRELAND
SIERRA LEONE
LIBERIA
CAPE VERDE IS.

from your little artist

- art on paper

companion art projects

- any drawing project
- watercolour painting
- monoprinting

STRING OF LANTERNS

Perfect for displaying any artwork on paper, the whole family can help fold paper lanterns to hang above a window or string across a room. For this project I photocopied some of Lily's monoprints, which she then painted to add some colour (a lovely alternative to the traditional colouring-in book).

What you need

- scissors, paper trimmer or guillotine
- needle and thread

What to do

Cut the artwork into squares, at least 15 cm × 15 cm (6 in × 6 in). You can use scissors; however, a paper trimmer or guillotine will give you the best results.

Follow the origami instructions below to make as many lanterns as you like. Every time you make a fold, run your fingernail along the folded edge to make a nice sharp crease.

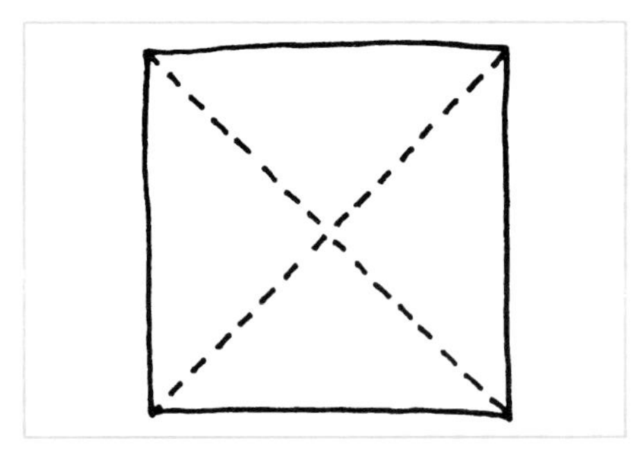

a Fold square diagonally to create a triangle. Unfold. Turn over and fold on the other diagonal. Unfold.

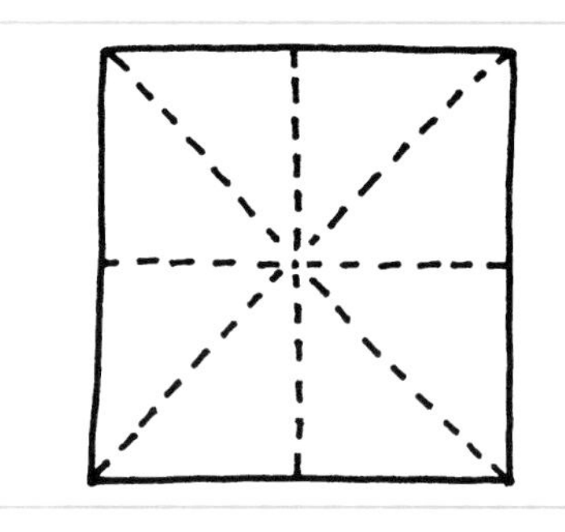

b Turn over and fold in half to create a rectangle. Unfold. Turn paper by 90 degrees and fold again.

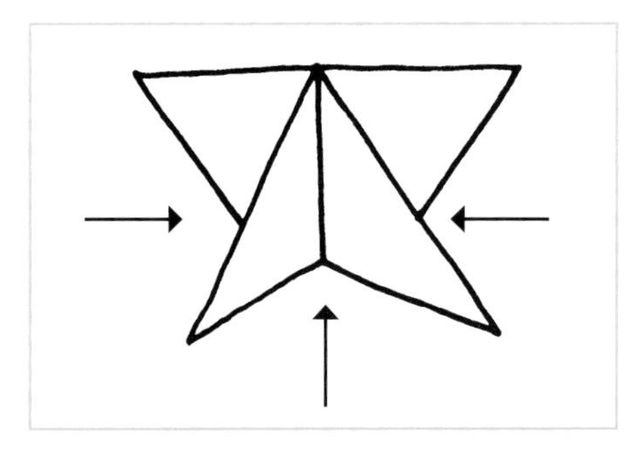

c Turn over and collapse the sides inwards so the folded paper makes a triangle shape.

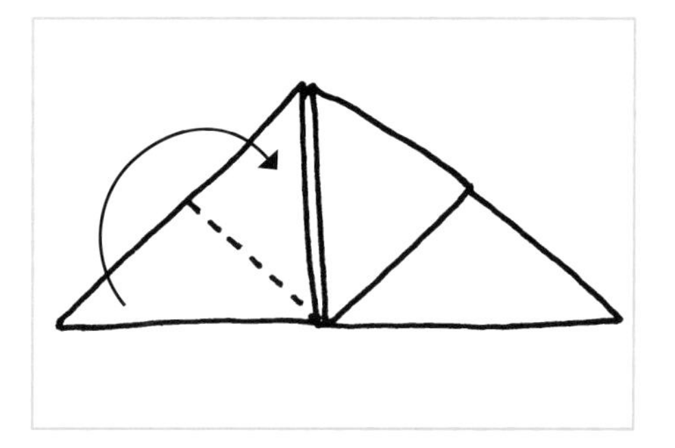

d Fold outer corners inward to make a square. Turn over and repeat.

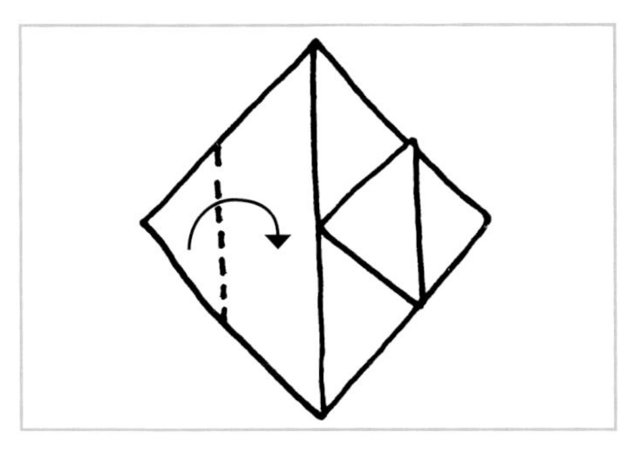

e Fold left and right corners into the centre. Turn over and repeat.

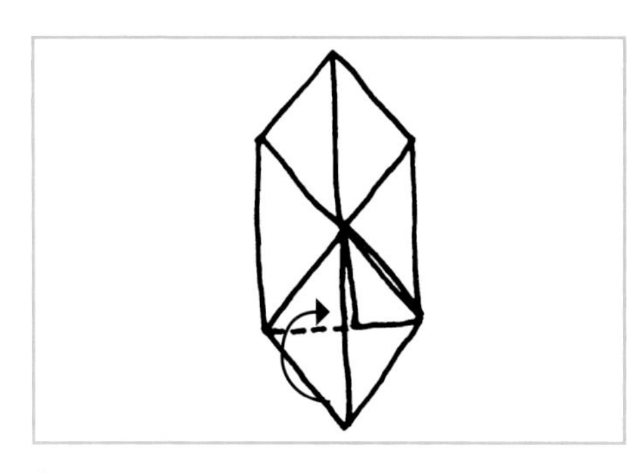

f Fold bottom corners into the centre. Turn over and repeat.

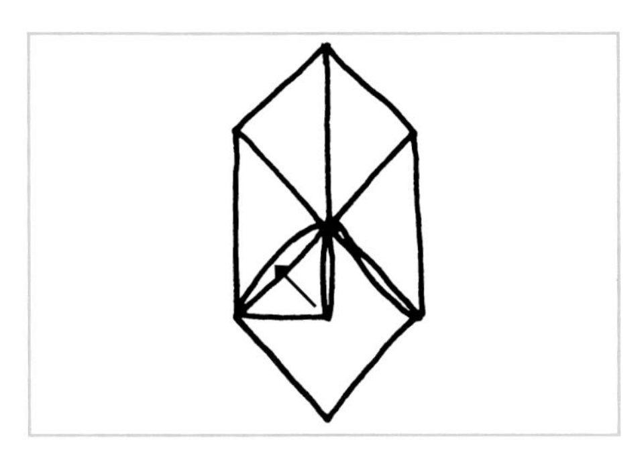

g With thumb and forefinger, open out the triangles formed in step **e** and tuck folded bottom corners inside. Turn over and repeat.

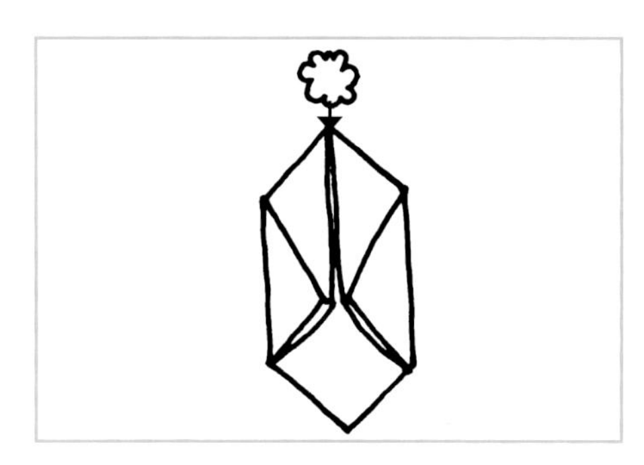

h Now expand the lantern by gently blowing into the hole at the top, just like a balloon!

3 Pierce the paper lanterns through the top with your needle, then pass onto the thread. Keep doing this until you've threaded all the lanterns – you can have them evenly spaced or let them dangle in random intervals. To stop your lanterns slipping along the thread, you can tie knots between each lantern as you are threading them on, or dab a little glue where the thread enters the hole in the lantern (be sure to let the glue dry before hanging).

tips + tricks

If you have some fairy lights, you can illuminate your lanterns – instead of stringing them onto thread, gently push the lanterns over the fairy light globes.

EMBROIDERED PLACEMAT

Make your child's art a feature at the dining-room table with this lovely placemat. Lily made a great drawing of our dog, Oscar (which you can see on page 18), who now joins us for dinner both on, and under, the table.

What you need

- traced Embroidered Placemat template (page 230)
- 14 cm × 21 cm (5½ in × 8¼ in) plain fabric for embroidery panel
- fabric pieces in complementary patterns and colours to sew around embroidery panel, to make a 32 cm × 25 cm (12½ in × 10 in) rectangle
- 32 cm × 25 cm (12½ in × 10 in) cotton fabric for the back
- 32 cm × 25 cm (12½ in × 10 in) quilt batting
- tracing paper
- transfer pencil
- small embroidery hoop (optional)
- basic sewing kit (page 65)

What to do

Trace your child's artwork onto tracing paper using a transfer pencil – make sure your design is the right size to fit piece 4A of the template. Iron the transfer onto the embroidery panel fabric, following the manufacturer's instructions – this provides you with a guide for your embroidery.

Stitch over the transfer lines using a sewing machine, or if you are hand-sewing, place the fabric in an embroidery hoop and use a simple straight stitch or back stitch (see page 72). You can make the embroidered design subtle by using a single thread like I have or you can double or triple the thread to make the embroidery really defined and bold.

Cut out the Embroidered Placemat template and pin the pieces to the fabric (use piece 4A to cut your embroidered piece).

Using the diagram on page 160 as a guide, make your patchwork. Always place right sides together and leave a 1 cm (⅜ in) seam allowance. It is also really helpful to iron the seams flat as you go.

What to do

Start by sewing piece 1A to piece 2A, then 2A to 3A, and so on until all of the A pieces are sewn together. Sew pieces 1B, 2B and 3B into a strip, and then sew the B pieces to the A pieces as shown on the template.

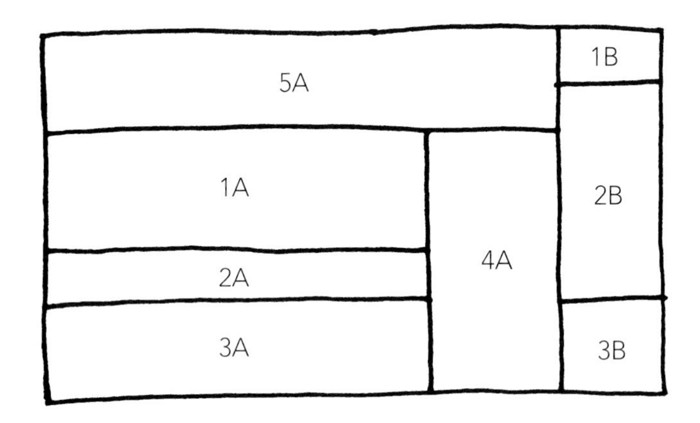

5. Place the patchwork front piece on top of the batting, right side facing up, then place the back piece on top, right side down. Pin together, placing some pins around the middle as well, so that the batting is nice and secure.

6. Sew all the way around the edges, using a 1 cm (3⁄8 in) seam allowance and leaving a 5 cm (2 in) opening on one side for turning the right way out. Be sure to back-stitch at the beginning and end so that the stitching doesn't come undone.

7. Turn right way out and press flat with an iron. Top-stitch all the way around the placemat, 2–3 mm (1⁄8 in) from the edge (this will stitch the opening closed).

8. Starting on one long edge, a few centimetres from the corner, top-stitch a vertical line across the placemat. When you get to the topstitching at the other side, put the sewing-machine needle down, lift the foot and turn the placemat 90 degrees. Lower the foot and stitch for a few centimetres (about an inch), then lift the foot again, turn the placemat 90 degrees and stitch vertically across the placemat, parallel to your first row of stitching (as shown in the diagram opposite). Continue in this way until you have quilted the whole placemat – just remember not to stitch over your embroidery!

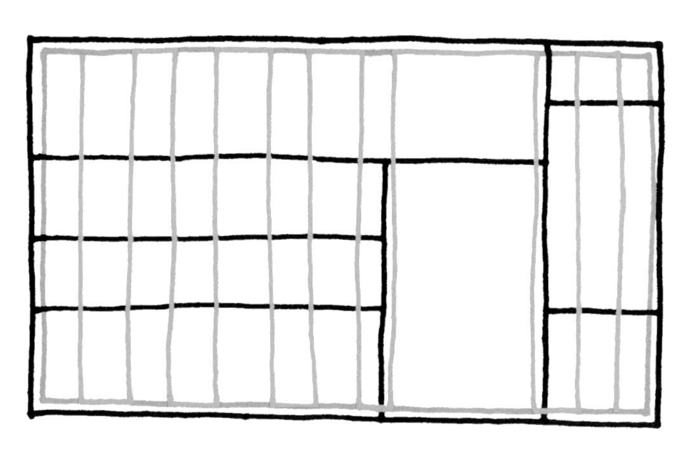

9 I made my rows of stitching about 3 cm (1¼ in) apart, but you can do more, or less, if you like.

tips + tricks

You can try out different fabric combinations for your patchwork by laying them all down on your table or floor and moving them around until you're happy with the arrangement. It can be a real challenge to match fabrics together to good effect. This is often the most time consuming part of patchwork and the most rewarding. Here are some tips for selecting and matching fabrics:

- choose a favourite fabric which has at least three colours in it, then find more fabrics with only those colours
- use my favourite rule: one spotted fabric, one striped fabric, one solid fabric, one open patterned fabric (lots of space between the designs) and one tightly patterned fabric
- if you don't have much choice or are still stuck, then grouping fabrics into a category will work really well. For example, only choose warm colours or only use one textile designer (they often use complimentary colour palettes).

from your little artist

- printed fabric

companion art projects

- faux lino printing
- screen printing
- Gocco printing

FABRIC WALL-HANGING

What better way to showcase your child's beautiful fabric prints than to mount them on canvas and hang them on a wall? I love doing a few of these on canvasses of the same size and hanging them in a line or grid.

What you need

- printed fabric
- stretched canvas – length and width will need to be about 20 cm (8 in) smaller than the piece of fabric
- staple gun and staples
- iron

tips + tricks

Folding the corners in is the trickiest part of this project – you may need to have a few tries before you can staple them down.

What to do

1. Iron your fabric so that it's nice and smooth.
2. Lay the fabric right side down on your work table and place the canvas face down on top. Trim the fabric so that there's a border of about 10 cm (4 in) around the canvas.
3. Fold the fabric over the middle of the top piece of the frame. Staple into place and, pulling firmly so that the fabric is taut, do the same on the other three sides.

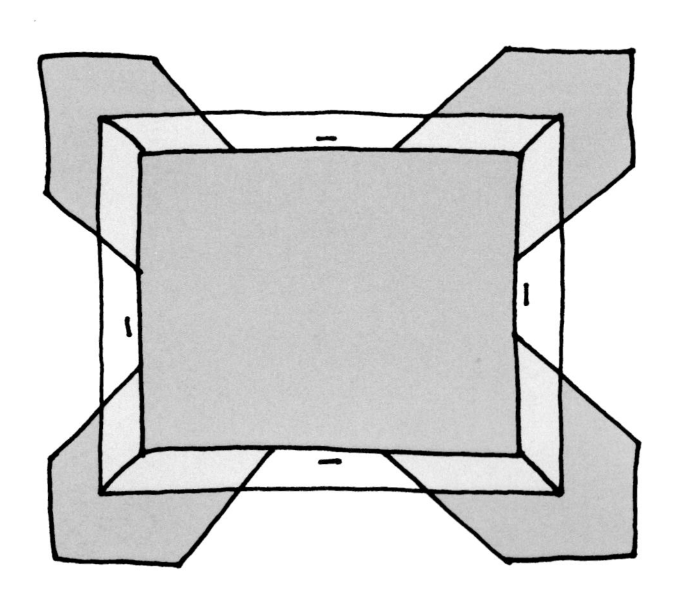

4 Working outwards from the centre staples, and keeping the fabric taut, staple the rest of the fabric down so that only the corners are left sticking out.

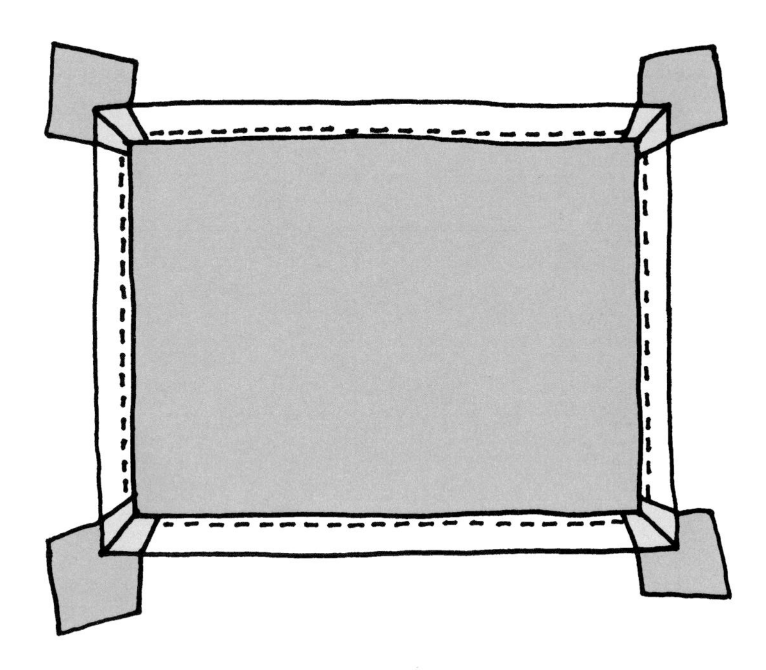

5 Take the tip of a fabric corner and fold it in over the corner of the frame, pushing the edges out so that it makes a square shape when it's folded down. Take the folded-over corners of the 'square' and fold inwards, one over the other. You should now have a nice neat corner which you can secure with a few staples. Do the same for the last three corners, and you have a beautiful artwork to hang on your wall.

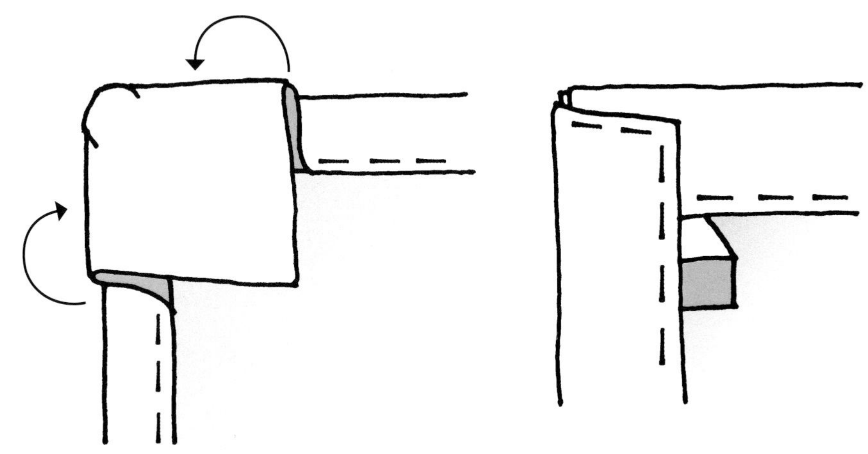

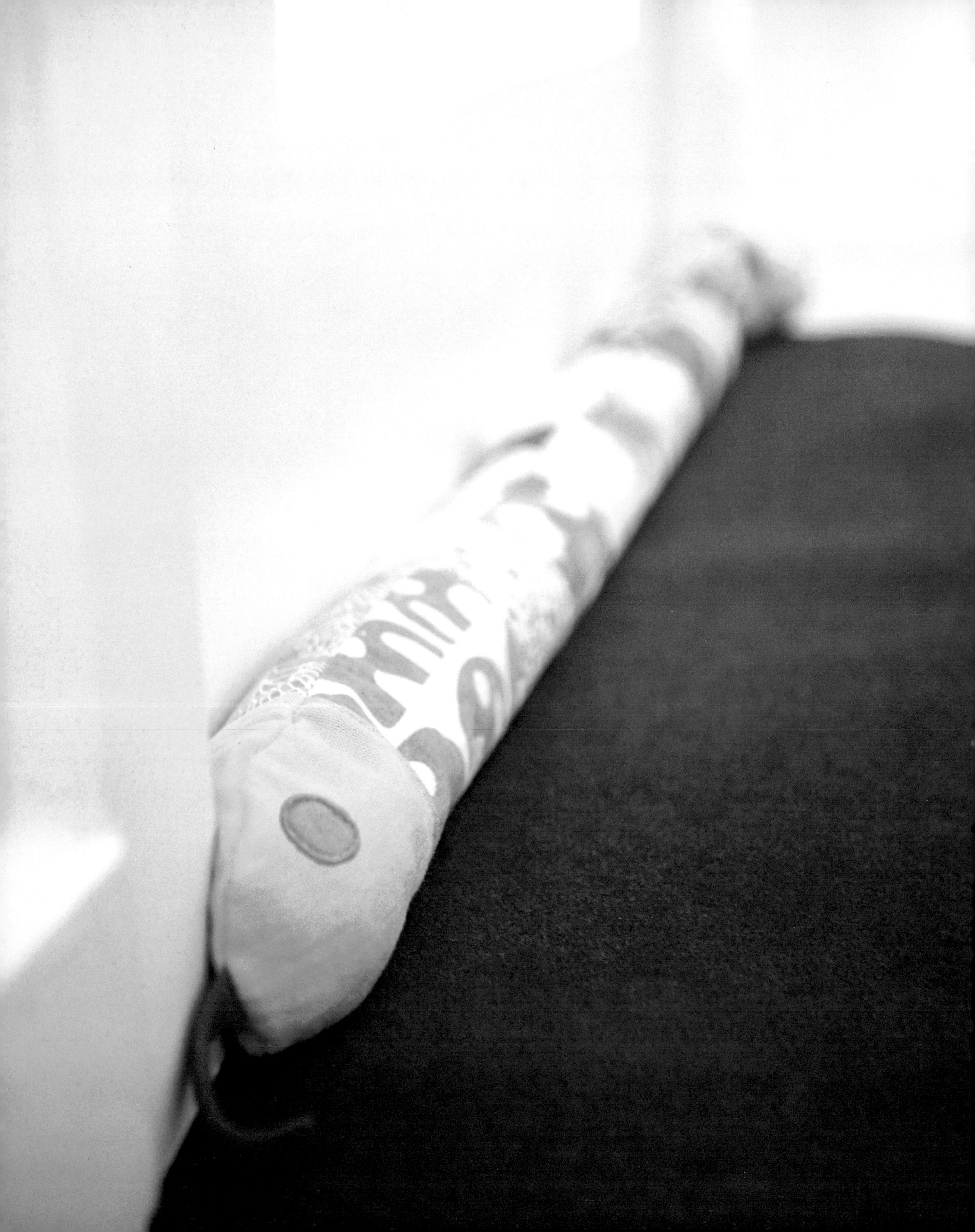

Draught stoppers, or 'door snakes', are really easy to make and so useful for keeping the heat (or cool) inside your house. Unfortunately, they're usually just boring tubes of fabric. Liven up your doorway with one of your child's favourite animal drawings – it could be a cheeky monkey, a dog, or an actual snake! Think of this project as making a soft toy with an elongated body.

What you need

- 100 cm × 24 cm (40 in × 9½ in) fabric for the body
- pieces of fabric for making the head and other body parts
- quilt batting
- polyester stuffing
- sand, aquarium gravel or kitty litter
- basic sewing kit (page 65)

What to do

1. For the main body of your draught-stopper creature, you'll need to cut your fabric into two rectangles, 12 cm (5 in) wide. To determine the length, measure along the bottom of your door, then add 5 cm (2 in). My door is 85 cm (33½ in) wide, so my body pieces were 90 cm × 12 cm (35½ in × 5 in).

2. Cut shapes out of your fabric scraps for a head and any other body parts pictured in your child's drawing, such as arms, legs, tails or spikes – just remember to cut two of each shape. You can create templates for these shapes by tracing your child's art onto tracing paper, or you can just use the artwork as a guide. Make sure the 'neck' of your head shape is 12 cm (5 in) wide, so that it will fit to the body piece.

3. Cut a piece of batting for each of these body-part shapes (excluding the head).

4. Place matching fabric body-part shapes with right sides together and put the batting on top. Stitch together, leaving the edges that will be attached to the body open. Turn right way out.

5. Sew the 'neck' of each head piece to one of the short ends of each body piece, right sides together.

6. Lay one of the long body pieces out flat on your table, right side facing up. Position all of your body-part pieces on top, lining up the raw edges so that the body parts are all pointing inwards to the body. Place the other long body piece on top, right side down, and carefully pin everything in place.

7. Starting at the corner of the short edge (at the tail end), sew all the way around the body and head until you get to the other side of the short edge, securing the body-part pieces as you go and leaving the end open. Turn right way out – you should have a long tube with all of the arms and legs dangling out.

8. Push polyester stuffing all the way along the tube into your creature's head until it is firmly stuffed. You will need to use something long to help you do this, such as a wooden spoon. Now you can decorate your creature's face using embroidery or appliqué – maybe sew on some buttons for the eyes.

9. Fill up the body of your creature with sand, kitty litter or aquarium gravel. I find a funnel is useful if you want to avoid pouring your filling everywhere. Be careful not to overfill the tube, as it can make this tricky to sew up. Stuff a little more polyester stuffing in the end to help avoid leaks.

10. Hand-sew the end closed using ladder stitch.

tips + tricks

You can also stuff your draft stopper with fabric. It's a great way of recycling fabric scraps and old clothing not fit for the op-shop.

Who wouldn't be excited about breakfast with these little cuties keeping your eggs warm? Animal pictures make particularly good inspiration for this project – I used Lily's painting of a whale, pictured on page 30 – but you can make these adorable cosies in any shape you like!

What you need

- traced Egg Cosy template (page 224)
- 15 cm (6 in) square of wool felt
- scraps of felt and fabric for decoration
- basic sewing kit (page 65)

What to do

The Egg Cosy template gives you the basic shape you'll need to cover an egg. Draw your own shape onto the tracing paper, using the template as a base.

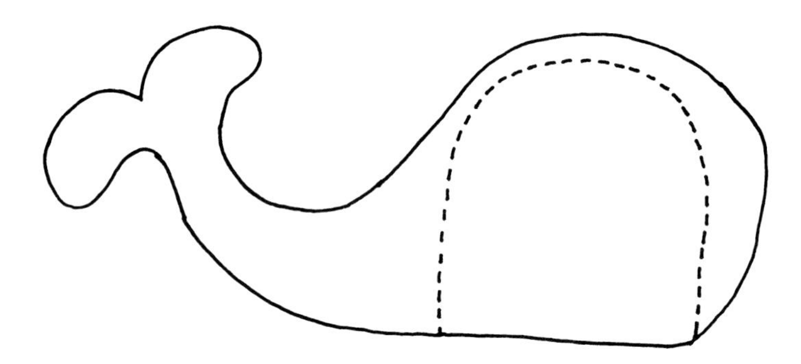

Fold the felt piece in half. Pin your tracing paper template to the felt and cut it out. If your cosy has any extra bits such as ears or a tail, cut them out now as well.

I find it's easier to do any embroidery or appliqué before sewing the felt pieces together. Stitch on a cute little face, some clothes, hair – whatever detail your cosy needs! Just remember, if you are decorating both sides, make sure your felt shapes are mirror-images of each other – I've lost count of the number of times I've gone to sew something together and realised I've done all of my beautiful embroidery on the wrong side of the fabric!

4. Pin the two felt pieces together, with the decorated sides facing in. If you have any pieces you want sticking out of your cosy (such as hair or horns), these need to be sandwiched between the two sides (if you were adding horns, for example, the bottom edges of the horns would need to line up with the outer edge of the cosy).

5. Using a sewing machine or needle and thread, sew the two felt pieces together. Make sure you leave a 5 cm (2 in) opening in the bottom edge of your cosy (as shown on the template), as this is where it goes over the egg.

6. Turn your cosy right side out (you may need a knitting needle to push out any tricky bits) and you're ready for breakfast!

tips + tricks

I just love soft-boiled eggs for breakfast! To make soft-boiled eggs, I put the eggs into a small saucepan of cold water over a high heat. As soon as the water boils, I reduce the heat to medium and then boil the eggs for one minute. And of course, I always serve my eggs with buttery toast cut into soldiers. Yum!

from your little artist

- art for tracing

companion art projects

- any art project

CUSHION CRITTER

Liven up your lounge room with this adorable cushion! I used Lily's drawing of our dog, Oscar, on page 18 as inspiration, so she can curl up with him on the couch even when he's playing outside.

What you need

- 50 cm (20 in) square of plain cotton fabric for the front
- 50 cm (20 in) square of patterned fabric for the back
- 20 cm × 50 cm (8 in × 20 in) fabric for the flap
- wool felt in colours to match your child's drawing
- embroidery needle and thread
- 50 cm (20 in) square cushion insert
- tracing paper
- transfer pencil
- embroidery hoop (optional)
- basic sewing kit (page 65)

What to do

1. Trace your child's artwork onto tracing paper using a transfer pencil. Iron the transfer onto the front fabric, following the manufacturer's instructions – this provides you with a guide for your appliqué and embroidery.

2. Cut out the appliqué shapes you've drawn on the tracing paper, pin them to the felt, and cut. Pin the felt pieces to the front fabric piece, using the transfer lines as a guide, and stitch on using a sewing machine or needle and thread. Stretch the fabric in an embroidery hoop if you are hand stitching – you can use straight stitch, back stitch or blanket stitch (see pages 72–3).

What to do *continued*

3. Embroider over any remaining transfer lines using straight stitch or back stitch (see page 72) – or you can cheat like me and use a sewing machine.

4. With right sides facing, stitch one edge of the front and back pieces together, leaving a 1 cm (3/8 in) seam allowance. Then stitch the flap to the opposite edge of your front piece so that you have one long strip.

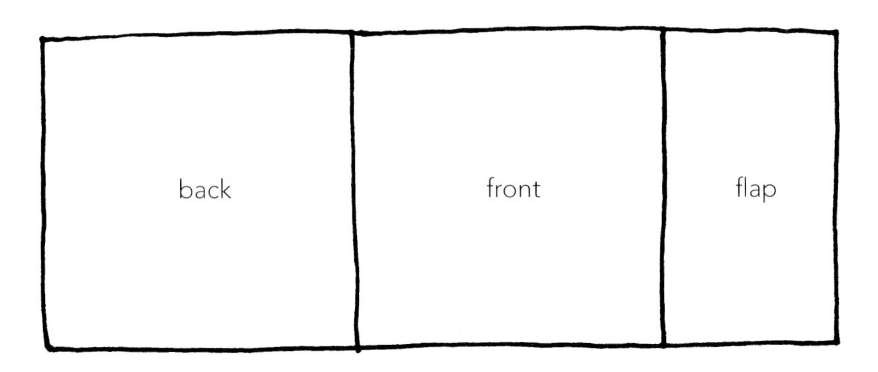

5. Hem the short ends of the strip by zigzag-stitching or overlocking the raw edges, folding over by 1 cm (3/8 in), ironing flat and then stitching.

6. Fold the flap over the front piece so that the wrong sides are facing. Fold the back piece over the front piece so that right sides are facing. Sew along the top and bottom raw edges leaving a 1 cm (3/8 in) seam allowance.

7 Turn the right way out – the cover should look just like a square pillowcase. Pop the cushion insert inside the cover and pull the flap over the insert to keep it in place.

tips + tricks

If you'd like to be a bit adventurous and add ears (or tails, or wings) to your cushion as I have, cut whatever shapes you'd like from your fabric, leaving a straight edge to match up with the side of your cushion. Before you sew the edges of your cushion together in step 6, position your shapes inside the front and back cushion-pieces, matching the straight edges with the cushion edges, and secure with pins. These pieces will be sewn into place when you stitch the cushion edges together, and will stick out from the seams once you turn your cushion the right way out.

TO GIVE

from your little artist

- a screen-printing stencil or Gocco screen

companion art projects

- screen printing
- Gocco printing

PRINTED NOTEBOOK

A notebook is such a handy thing to have. I carry one with me at all times – you never know when you'll think up a brilliant idea and need to write it down or make a quick sketch. Many notebooks are plain and boring – so why not print your own?

What you need

- materials for screen printing (page 48) or Gocco printing (page 54)
- plain notebook (cardboard or fabric covers work best)

What to do

1. Place your notebook on a flat surface with the front cover facing up.
2. Lay the stencil down in the desired position (skip this if you are using a Gocco screen) and place the screen on top. Plop a generous amount of ink across the top of the screen and drag the squeegee firmly over the screen towards you (for more detailed instructions see page 48 or 54).
3. Gently peel the screen off the printed surface (you may need to hold the notebook down so that it doesn't shift and smudge). Allow to dry as per the ink instructions.

tips + tricks

If you have a large stencil, you can print a bunch of notebooks in one go. Lay them out so that they fit under the screen, then print! This will create interesting shapes as only part of the design will fit on each journal.

These lovely boxes are easy to make and they're perfect for storing little things like jewellery or sewing notions. They also make beautiful gift boxes!

What you need

- scissors, paper trimmer or guillotine

What to do

Cut the artwork into squares (make them at least 15 cm × 15 cm, otherwise the folding can become rather tricky). You can use scissors; however, a paper trimmer or guillotine will give you the best results.

Follow the origami instructions below to make as many boxes as you like. Every time you make a fold, run your fingernail along the folded edge to make a nice sharp crease.

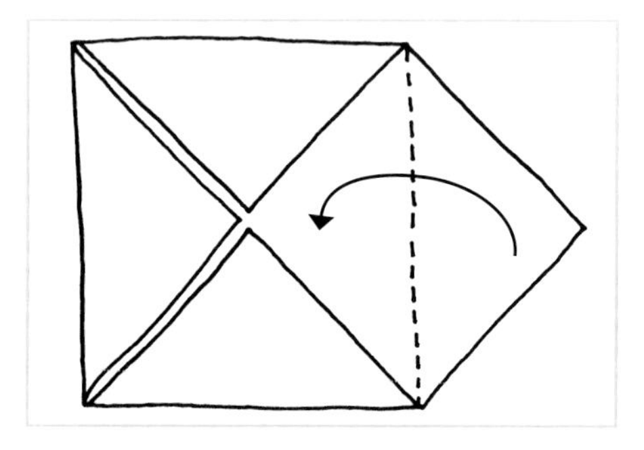

a Fold the four corners of the paper into the centre.

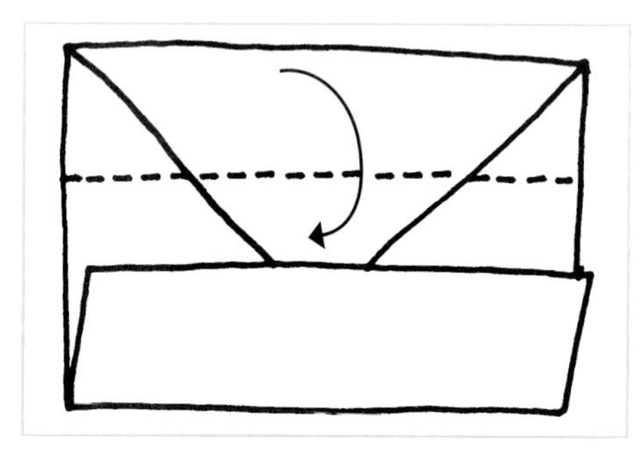

b Fold the top edge and the bottom edge into the centre to create a rectangle.

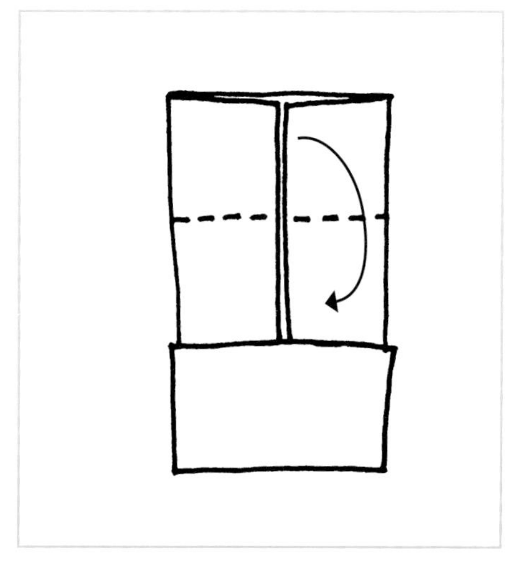

c Repeat with the side edges to make a square.

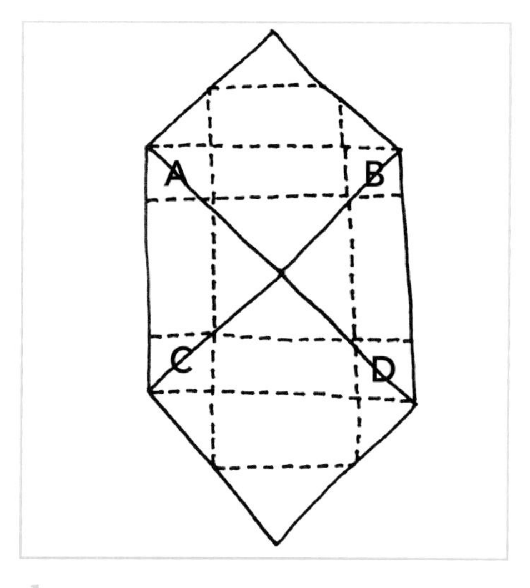

d Unfold, leaving the side corners still folded into the middle as shown.

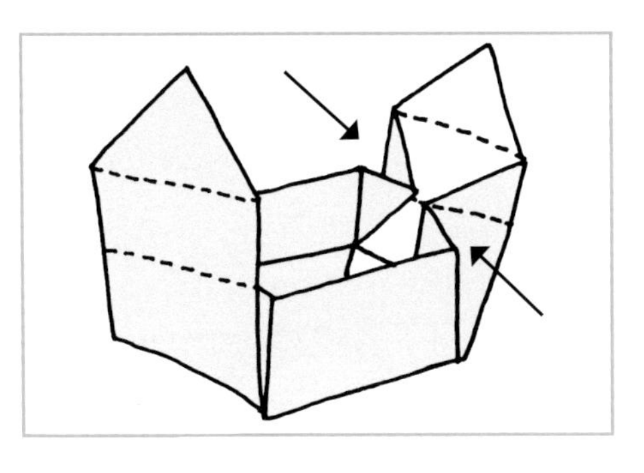

e Place your fingers underneath points A and B so the edges fold in. Repeat with points C and D.

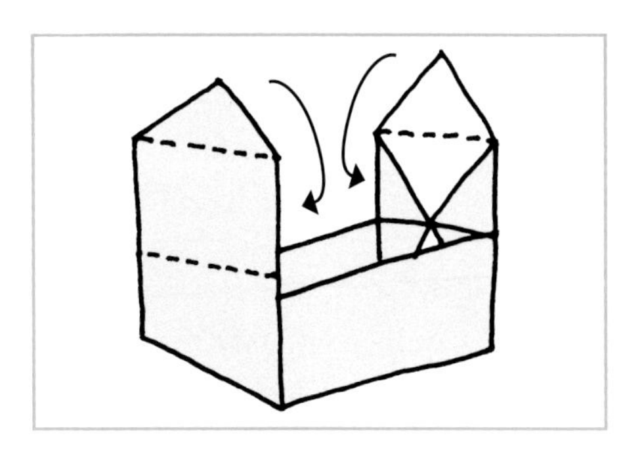

f Now fold the long ends in and over so that the corners all meet in the centre.

3 Follow the instructions above to make the lid, but start with a square of paper that is 5 mm (¼ in) bigger than the previous one so that the lid will fit over the top.

tips + tricks

I love using these as gift boxes for tiny presents – just place a little cotton wool in the bottom of the box and put your gift on top, then pop on the lid and secure with some ribbon!

from your little artist

- art for tracing

companion art projects

- any art project

Decorate a window, doorway, or even a Christmas tree with these lovely textural felt designs. These look so pretty in contrasting colours, or you could use several different shades of the one colour. I traced these beautiful shapes from Lily's monoprint on page 38.

What you need

- wool felt in various colours
- tracing paper
- pencil
- scissors
- sewing machine or needle and thread

What to do

1. Trace your child's artwork onto tracing paper using a pencil, then cut out the shapes to use as templates. It's best to use a piece of art that features big bold shapes without too much detail.

2. Pin the template pieces to the felt and cut out. Cut the shape or shapes from at least two different felt colours.

3. Decide what order you want your coloured felt layers to be in, then trim each shape (except the bottom one), so that each layer is 1–2 mm (⅛ in) smaller than the one below it.

4. Secure the layers with a pin, then stitch it all together with a sewing machine, or by hand using a straight stitch or back stitch (see page 72). You can just stitch around the edge of the top piece, or you can use stitching to add more detail and texture to the decoration – for example, by sewing criss-crossing lines for a quilted effect, or adding the veins onto a leaf shape.

5. Now you have your decoration, you just have to decide how to display it! You can thread a few of them onto a length of cotton or fishing line to hang over a door frame, or stitch a loop of ribbon onto the back of each one to make Christmas tree decorations. They also make brilliant gift wrapping – use some coloured thread to tie them on.

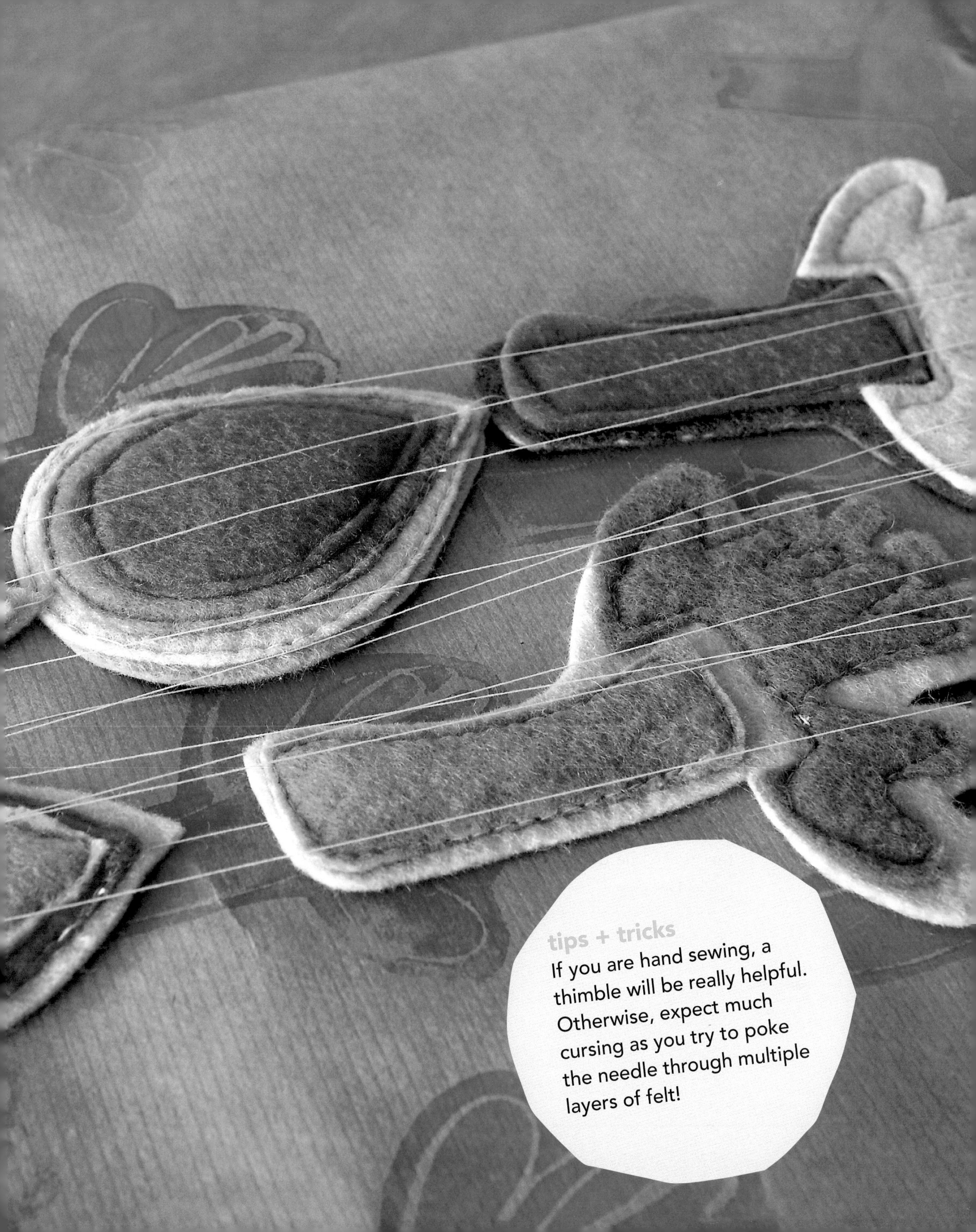

tips + tricks

If you are hand sewing, a thimble will be really helpful. Otherwise, expect much cursing as you try to poke the needle through multiple layers of felt!

lollies

from your little artist

- art for making a digital copy (see page 63)

companion art projects

- any art project

Use these gorgeous labels to organise your pantry, to indentify your child's art-making materials, or as gift tags! I made these cute dino-labels from Lily's screenprint on page 46.

What you need

- computer and printer or custom-made rubber stamp and ink pad
- sticky labels suitable for a printer, or matte-finish stickers for stamping

What to do

Computer

You will probably need to resize the digital copies of your child's images for them to fit the labels. You can also add text or borders – whatever you like! Make sure the image looks crisp and has a fair amount of contrast, otherwise the label will looked washed out.

Copy and paste your label image into Word or other word-processing program. You will need to set up your document with a table or template so that your image fits the label size when you print. Many of the label brands have free templates you can download from their website.

Pop your labels into the printer, press print, and presto! Beautiful labels ready for sticking.

Rubber stamp

First, ink the stamp using an ink pad. It doesn't matter what size ink pad you have because you can ink the stamp by dabbing it with the ink pad, rather than the other way round. This prevents the ink from pooling into the gaps and means you can ink up quite large stamps.

Lay your sticker sheets on a flat surface and stamp away! When stamping, use your palms and body weight to press down firmly and evenly (no rocking or rubbing, as this can smudge the work). Before you do your next stamp, check to see that the ink hasn't pooled into the gaps and if it has, gently wipe it off.

tips + tricks

You can have rubber stamps custom-made quite cheaply and easily – there are many services online, or you can order them through an office-supply store.

LYRA Super FERBY 90018

from your little artist

- a printing stencil or Gocco screen

companion art projects

- faux lino printing
- screen printing
- gocco printing

LETTER SET

This letter set makes such a beautiful gift, particularly for a proud grandparent, aunty or uncle. You could also adapt this project to make beautiful party invitations.

What you need

- 10 sheets of A4 paper
- 5 envelopes
- materials for faux lino printing (page 44), screen printing (page 48) or Gocco printing (page 54)
- 45 cm × 4 cm (18 in × 1½ in) strip of paper
- sticky tape
- A4-sized cellophane bag

What to do

To decorate your pages and envelopes, follow the instructions for faux lino printing (page 44), screen printing (page 48) or Gocco printing (page 54). Make sure you print in a corner or across the top or bottom of the pages – you have to leave room for letter-writing!

Using the long strip of paper, create a paper band to use as a label for your letter set. I designed mine on the computer, but you could decorate by hand using pen or texta or a custom-made stamp.

Once your prints are dry, neatly assemble your envelopes and sheets of paper. Wrap the paper band around them and secure the ends with some sticky tape. Slip your letter set into the cellophane bag, and it's ready for writing those lovely letters!

tips + tricks

I love using postconsumer-waste paper for this project – the texture really adds to the handmade quality and the colour looks particularly great with white ink.

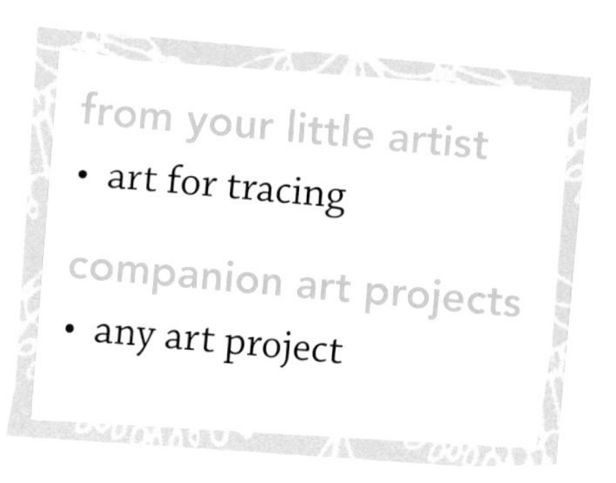

Turn a sketchbook or journal into a treasured gift with this easy sewing project – I replicated Lily's drawing on page 16 to make a travel journal. You can make the embroidery and appliqué as elaborate, or simple, as you like.

What you need

- Sketchbook Cover template (page 232)
- 23 cm × 60 cm (9 in × 23½ in) plain cotton fabric (or use fabric scraps sewn together) for the front
- 23 cm × 60 cm (9 in × 23½ in) patterned cotton fabric for the lining
- scraps of wool felt in colours to match your child's artwork
- 30 cm (12 in) twill tape or ribbon
- A5 sketchbook
- embroidery hoop (optional)
- tracing paper
- transfer pencil
- basic sewing kit (page 65)

What to do

1. If you are using a selection of fabric scraps for your front (as I did), sew them together with right sides facing, so that you end up with a piece no smaller than 23 cm × 60 cm (9 in × 23½ in). You can use different coloured and patterned fabrics here to replicate the background of your child's drawing.

2. Photocopy and cut out the Sketchbook Cover template. Place the front fabric and lining fabric right sides together and pin the template to the fabric. Mark the dots from the template onto one of your fabric pieces using tailor's chalk, then cut around the template.

3. Trace your child's artwork onto tracing paper using a transfer pencil. Iron the transfer onto the front fabric, following the manufacturer's instructions – this provides you with a guide for your appliqué and embroidery.

tips + tricks

The pattern provided is for an A5 sketchbook. If your book is a different size, simply open out the sketchbook, trace around the outside, then add 15 cm to each end for the flaps. Remember to leave a 5 mm (¼ in) seam allowance all the way around, and put a slight taper on the flap at the back.

What to do *continued*

4. Cut out the appliqué shapes you traced onto the tracing paper, pin them to the felt and cut out. Pin the felt pieces to the front fabric piece, using the transfer lines as a guide, and stitch on using a sewing machine or needle and thread. Stretch the fabric in an embroidery hoop if you are hand stitching – you can use straight stitch, back stitch or blanket stitch (see pages 72–3).

5. Embroider over any remaining transfer lines using straight stitch or back stitch – or you can use a sewing machine.

6. Pin the twill tape or ribbon to the right side of the lining fabric, as shown on the pattern. Now pin the lining and front fabric pieces together, right sides facing (the twill tape will be sandwiched between the two). Leaving a 5 mm (¼ in) seam allowance, sew all the way around the edges, starting at one of the opening marks and stopping at the other. Turn the right way out and use a knitting needle or chopstick to push the corners out.

7. Neatly iron the edges flat. With the cover lining side up on your ironing board, open out your sketchbook and place it in the middle of the cover. Fold the ends of the fabric cover over the sketchbook front and back covers so that the fabric fits nicely around the sketchbook. Slip the sketchbook out without disturbing the folds, and iron once more.

8. Ladder stitch (page 72) the top and bottom edges of the non-tapered flap to the front of the cover to create a pocket (stitching up the opening in the process). Slip the front cover of the sketchbook into the pocket and the back cover under the twill tape, then tuck the tapered flap under the twill tape to secure.

from your little artist

- art for tracing

companion art projects

- any art project

tips + tricks

When choosing an artwork to trace, pick something with a nice bold shape, that isn't too detailed, or else your stencil will become very fiddly to cut out.

GIFT CARDS

Everyone appreciates a handmade card – they're so much more personal than something hastily picked off a shelf in a shop. I like to make a bunch of these in one go so that I always have a supply of beautiful cards at home.

What you need

- cardstock (cut and folded into desired card size and shape)
- materials for screen printing (page 48)
- tracing paper
- pencil
- scissors

What to do

1. Trace your child's artwork onto tracing paper using a pencil, then cut out the design with the scissors.
2. Place the stencil in the desired position on the card and place the screen on top. Plop a generous amount of ink across the top of the screen and drag the squeegee firmly over the screen towards you (for more detailed instructions, see page 48).
3. Gently peel the screen off the printed surface (you may need to hold the card down flat so that it doesn't shift and smudge). Allow to dry as per the ink instructions.

Receiving a gift that is beautifully wrapped can sometimes be just as exciting as finding out what's inside. This super-simple project is a brilliant way to personalise a present.

What you need

- photocopier
- sticky tape (optional)

What to do

1. Take your child's art to your local office-supply shop or library and photocopy it onto A3 paper. You can use coloured paper for added effect or enlarge the image to make interesting designs. It's that simple!

2. If the gift you need to wrap is larger than what your A3 paper will cover, then make multiple copies and stick the pieces together with sticky tape.

3. I keep a supply of this homemade wrapping in the cupboard at home, as you never know when the opportunity to give someone something special will arise.

tips + tricks

Be extra-creative and complement your beautiful handmade paper with lovely decorations: tie ribbon, twine, raffia, crêpe paper or even strips of fabric around your gift; and find pretty, colourful objects to attach to the ribbons, such as leaves, plastic bottle caps, buttons or flowers from the garden. You could also use handmade stickers (page 89) or a felt decoration (page 191) and coloured thread to secure the wrapping paper, instead of using sticky tape.

LiLYS STiTCH iT KiT
Pattern + Fabric + Threads included

from your little artist

- art for making a digital copy (see page 63)

companion art projects

- any drawing project
- monoprinting
- watercolour painting

STITCH KIT

Give this kit as a gift to the crafter who has everything. Once they have stitched it all together they can use it to create any number of pretty items, such as a cushion cover or a panel on an apron.

What you need

- black and white reversed copy of your child's artwork (see page 63)
- colour copy of your child's artwork
- piece of plain loose-weave fabric (such as linen or hemp), a little larger than the artwork
- tracing paper
- transfer pencil
- iron
- cardboard
- embroidery thread to match the colours in the artwork
- embroidery needle
- pieces of felt to match the colours in the artwork
- embroidery hoop
- cellophane

What to do

1. Trace the reversed copy of your child's drawing onto tracing paper with a transfer pencil. Pin the tracing paper face down to the fabric square then iron over it with a dry iron. Unpin the tracing paper, fold the fabric neatly, and carefully secure the embroidery needle into the fabric.

2. Cut some thread cards out of cardboard – these are usually rectangles which are a little wider at the ends than they are in the middle, but you can be creative with the shapes. You can also draw pretty designs on them if you like. You will need one card for each thread colour. Cut a little snip in the top of each card. Now wind a few metres of embroidery thread onto each card, securing the end of the thread in the little snip in the top.

3. Lay a sheet of clear cellophane on your work surface and place the colour copy of your child's drawing on top, facing down. Neatly pile the fabric, felt pieces, embroidery hoop and thread cards on top and then wrap in cellophane.

4. With any leftover cardboard, make a label for the stitch kit. Decorate the label as you wish and then attach it neatly to the top of the cellophane wrapping.

tips + tricks

You can include some shapes cut out of felt to make an appliqué kit.

LILY

TEMPLATES

Puzzle Piece

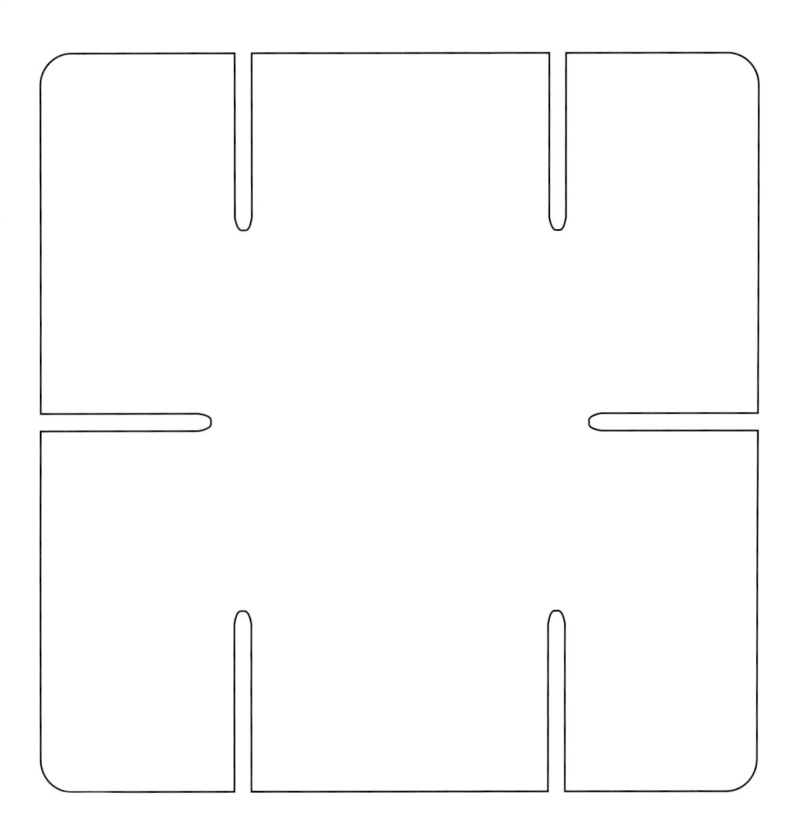

Art Smock

Enlarge by 200% for small, 250% for medium and 300% for large

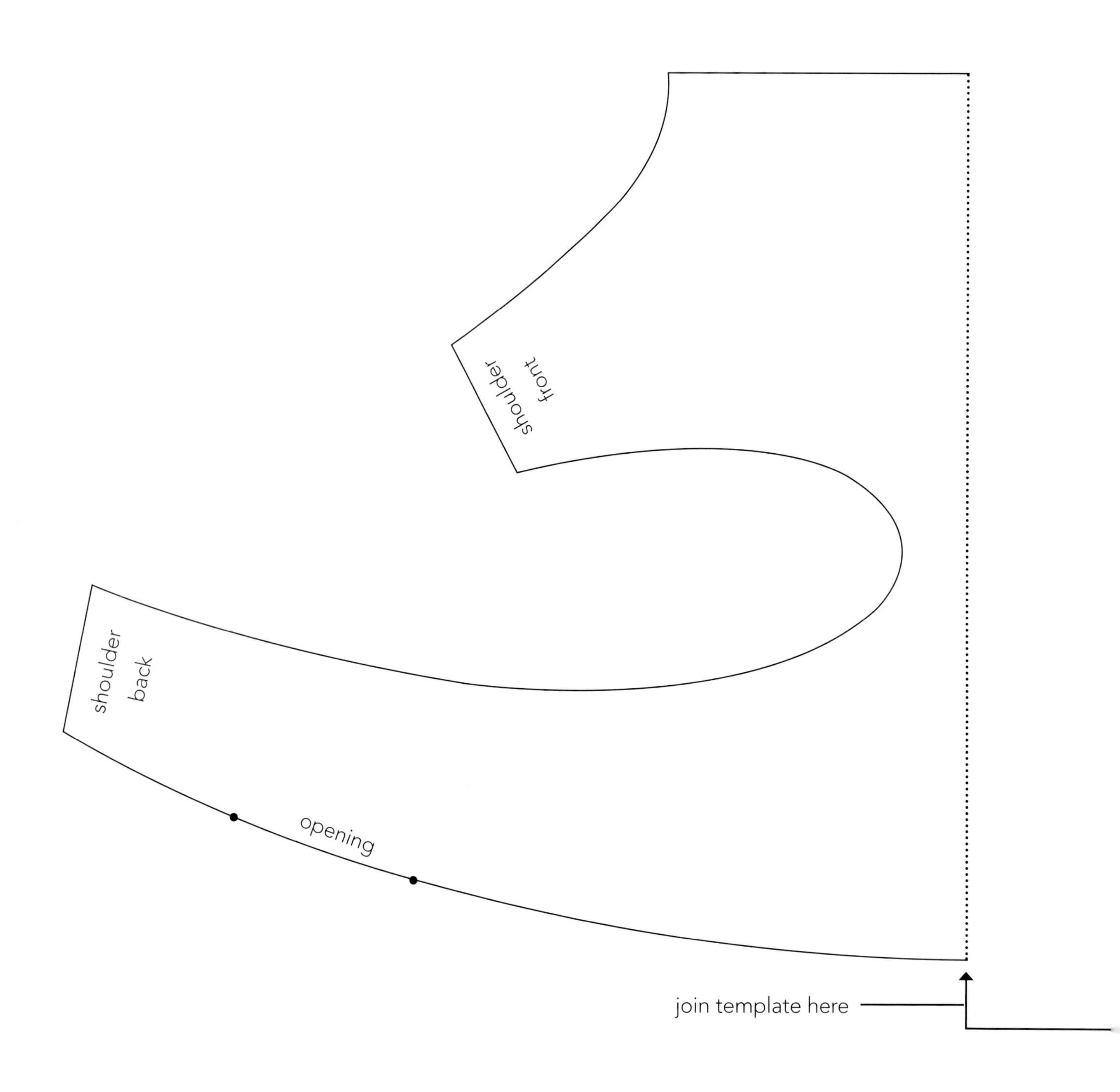

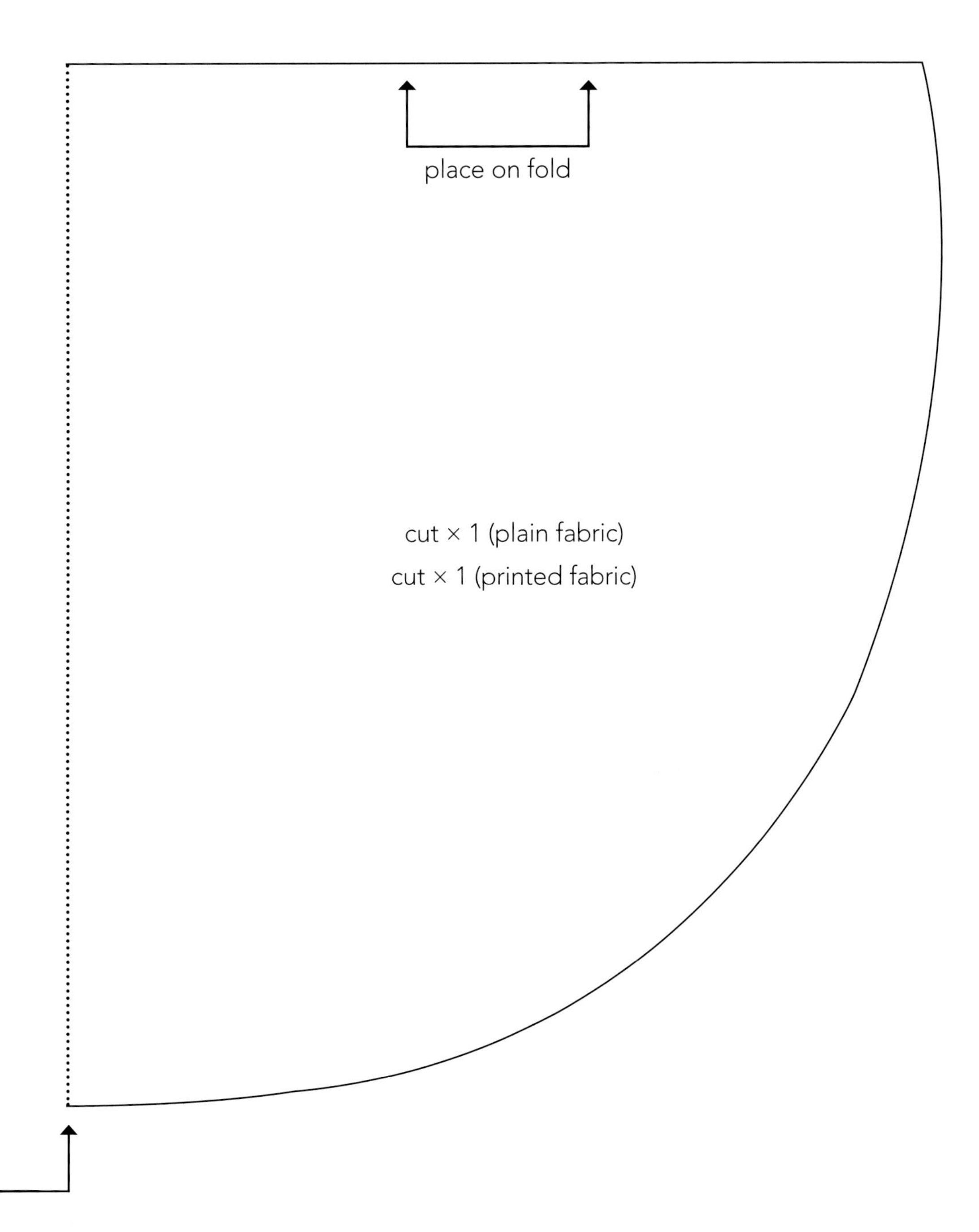
place on fold
cut × 1 (plain fabric)
cut × 1 (printed fabric)

Frenchy Scarf

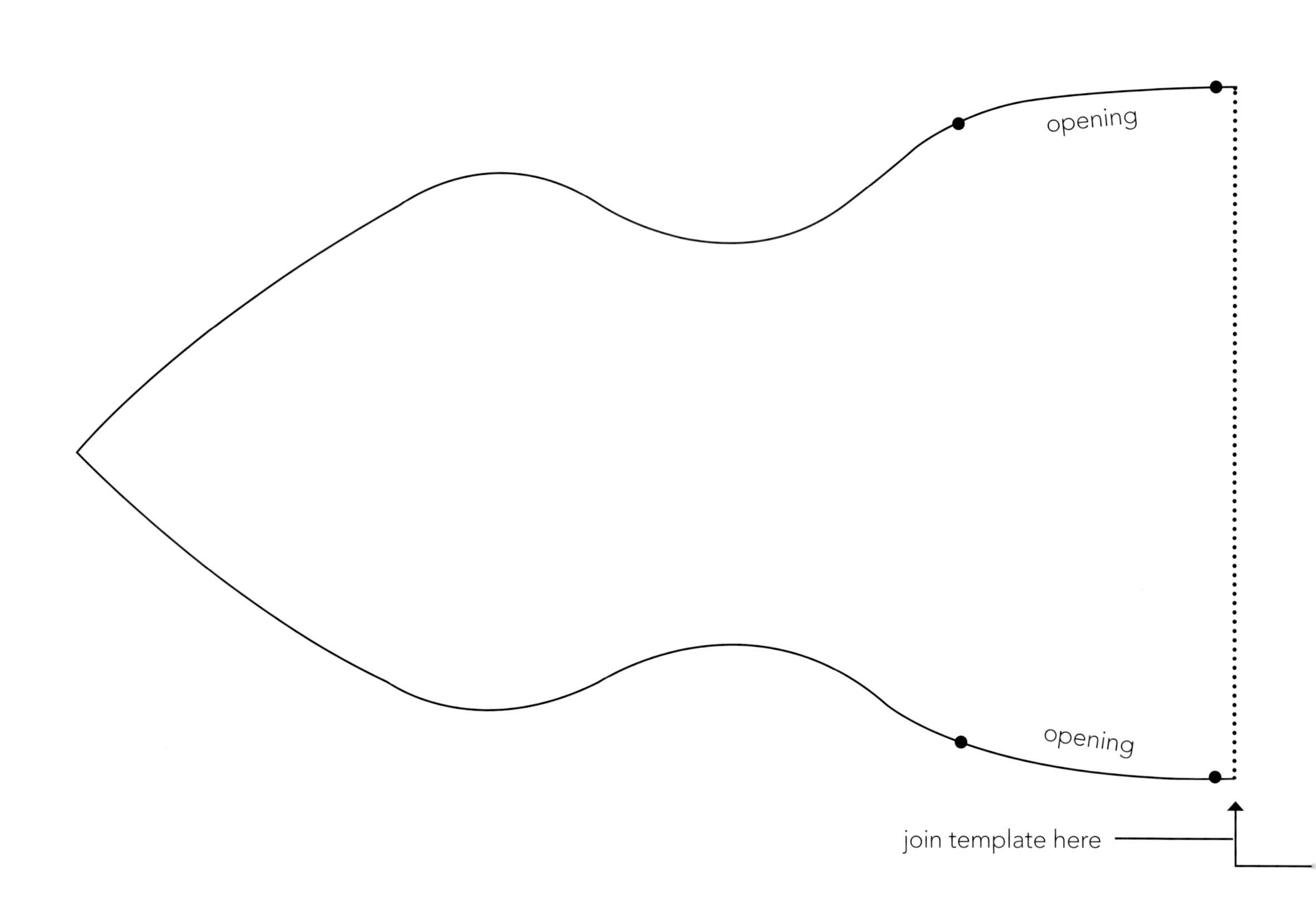

place on fold

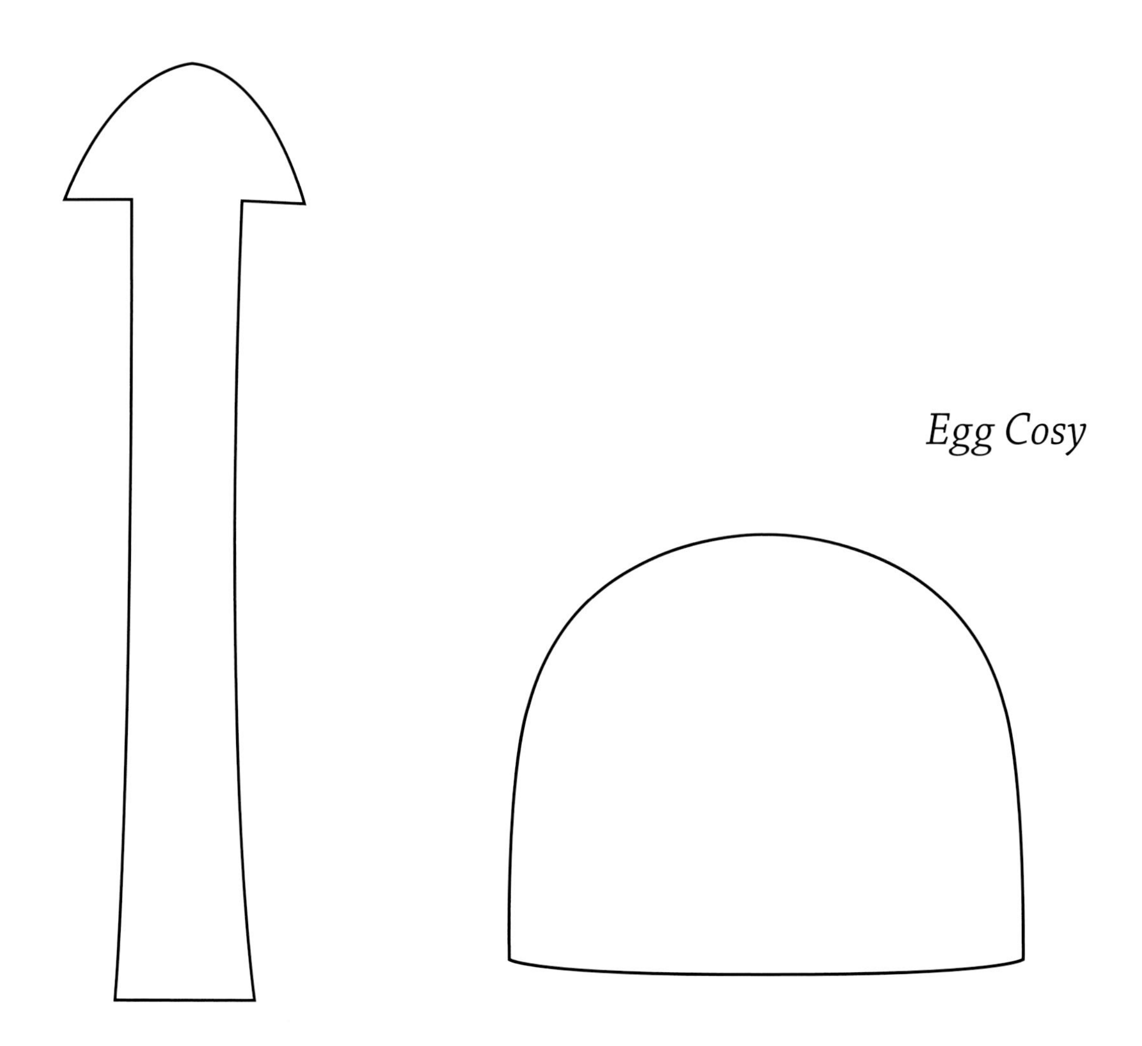
Bag Tag
Egg Cosy

Folk Handbag

Enlarge by 250%

Side A

cut × 2 (outer fabric)

cut × 2 (lining)

fold here

Handle loop

cut × 2 (outer fabric)

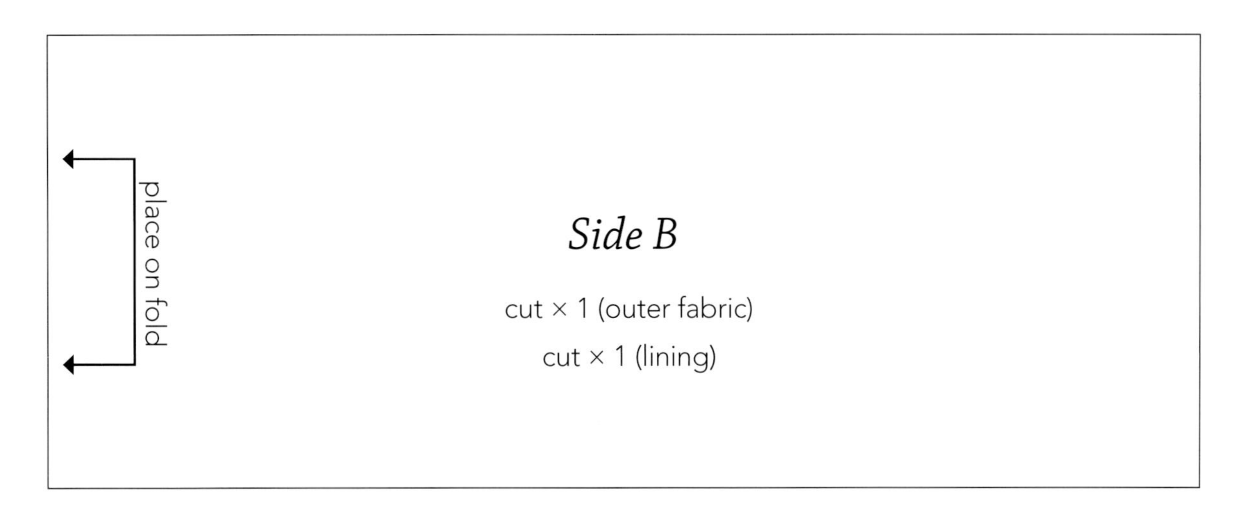

Side B

cut × 1 (outer fabric)

cut × 1 (lining)

Sunny Hat

Enlarge by 200% for small,
250% for medium and 300% for large

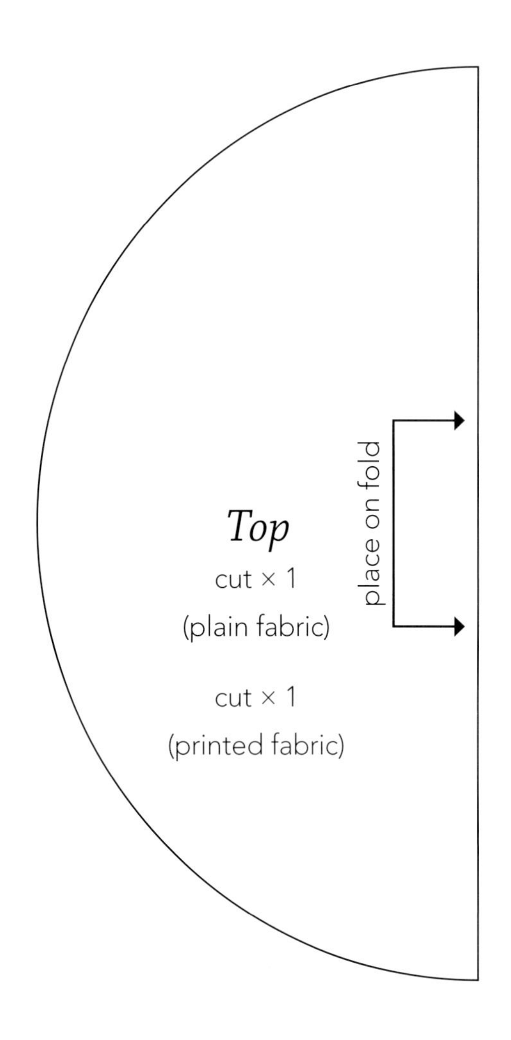

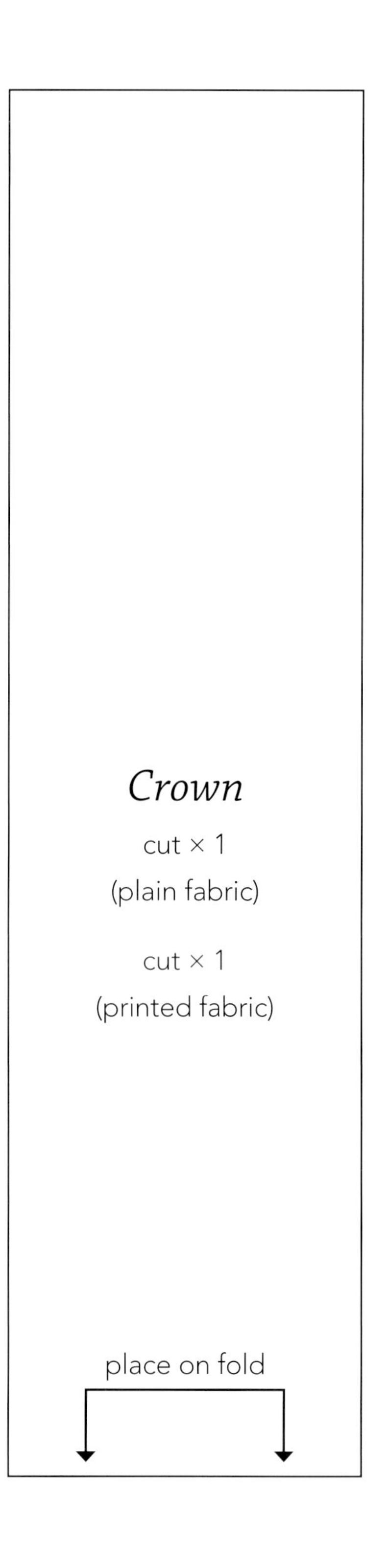

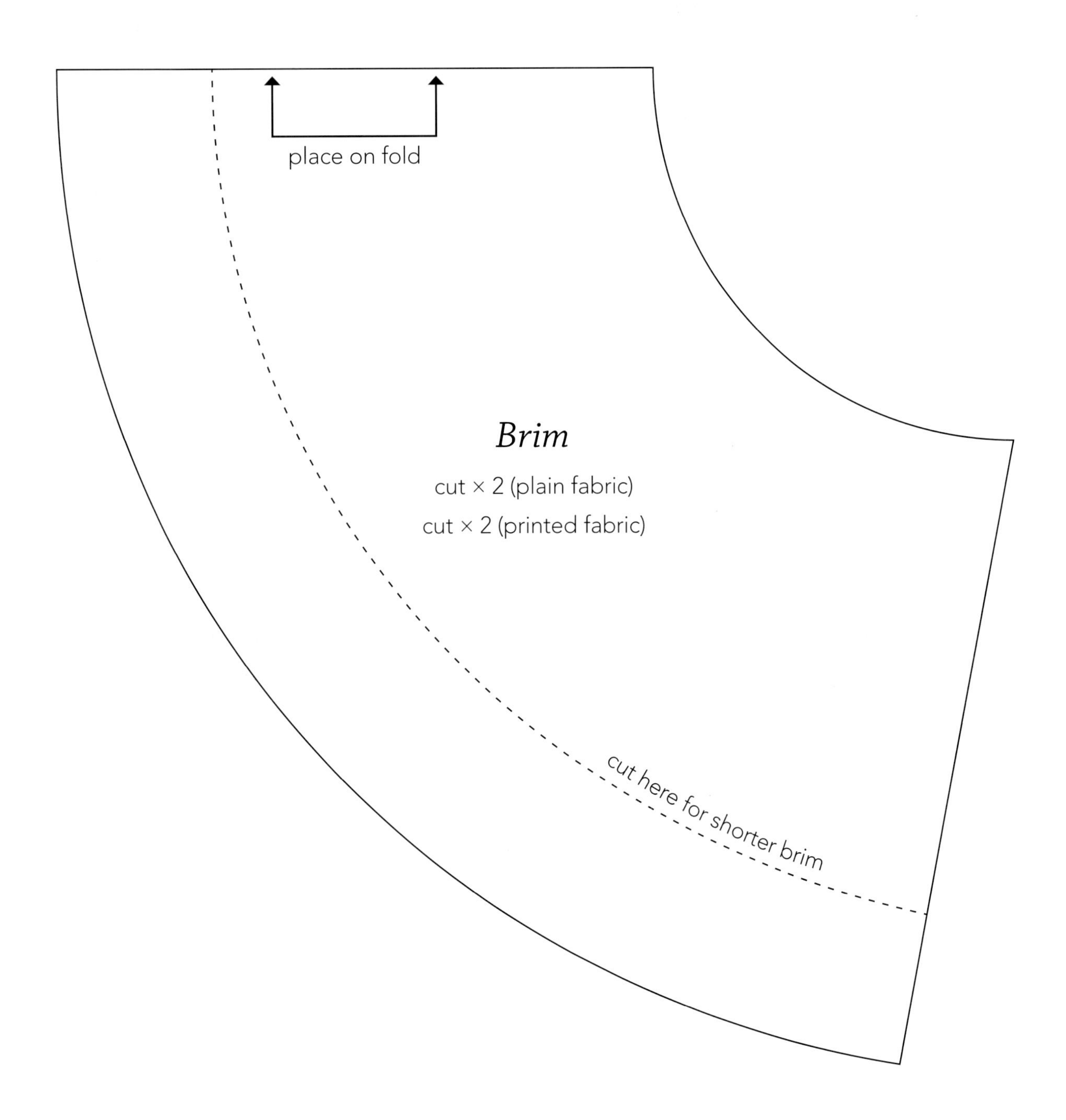
place on fold
Brim
cut × 2 (plain fabric)
cut × 2 (printed fabric)
cut here for shorter brim

Patchwork Cushion

Enlarge by 300%

1

2

4

3

5

6

7

8

9

10

11

12

13

Embroidered Placemat

Enlarge by 200%

1A

2A

3A

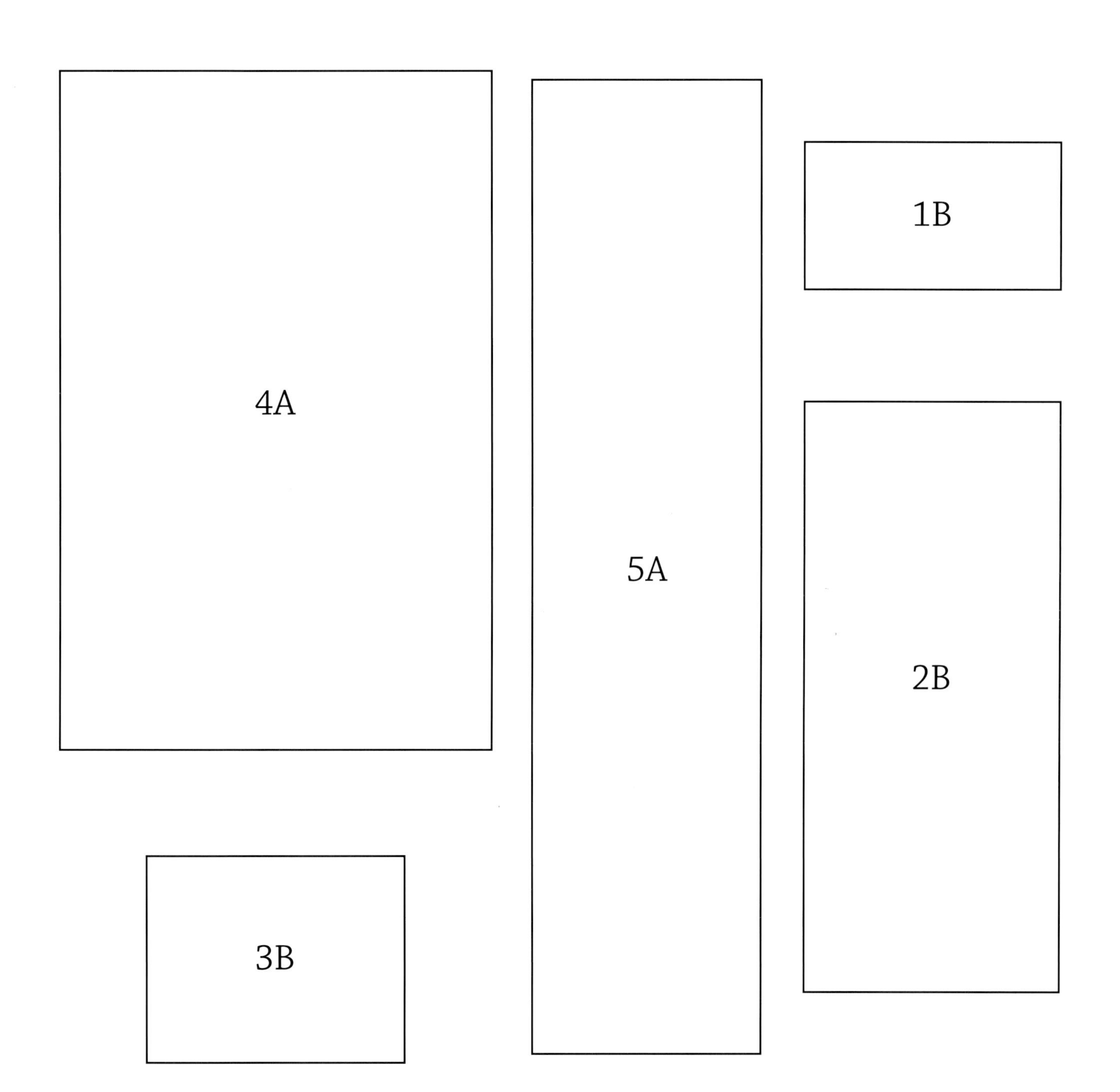
4A
5A
1B
2B
3B

Sketchbook Cover

Enlarge by 200%

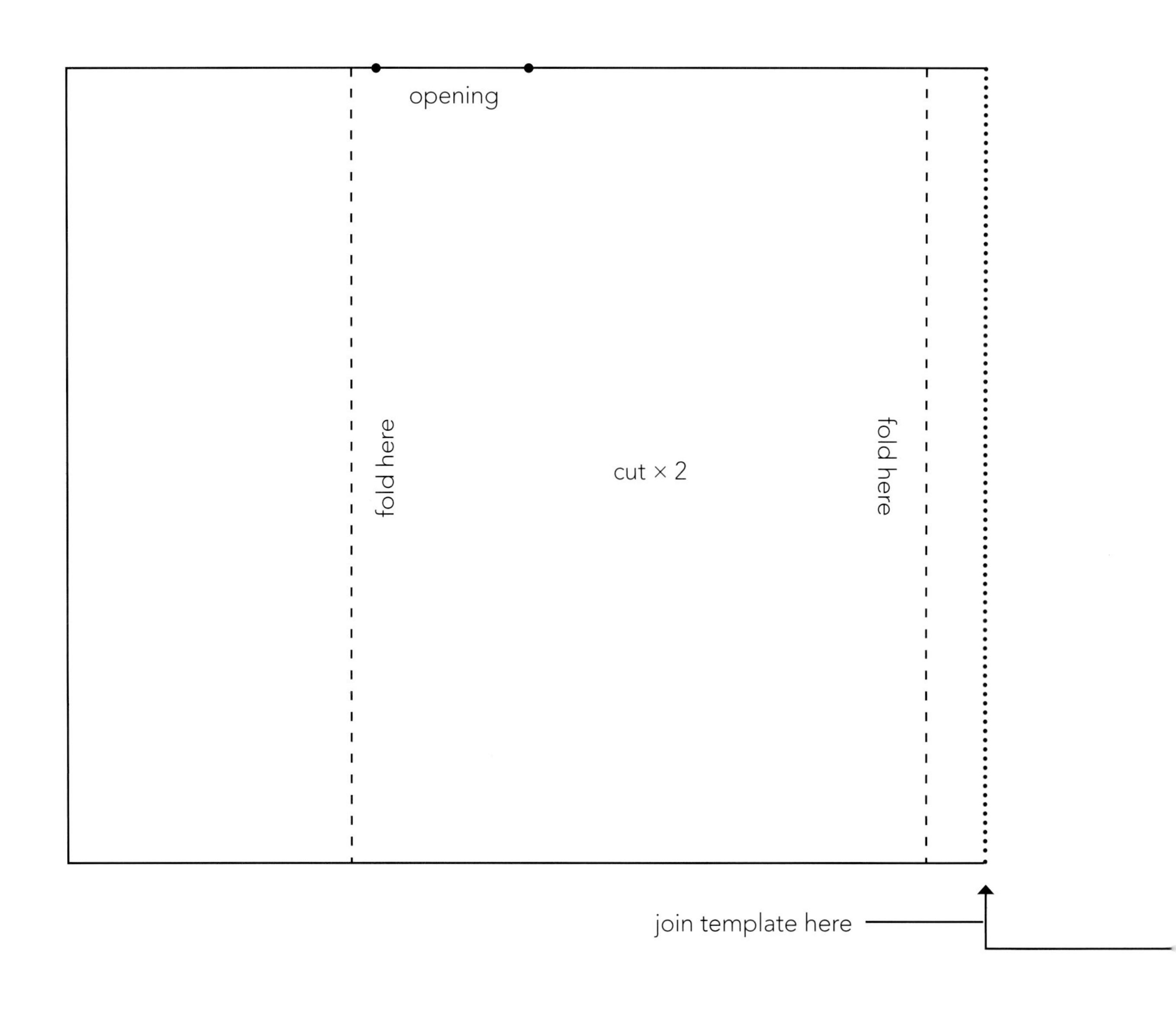

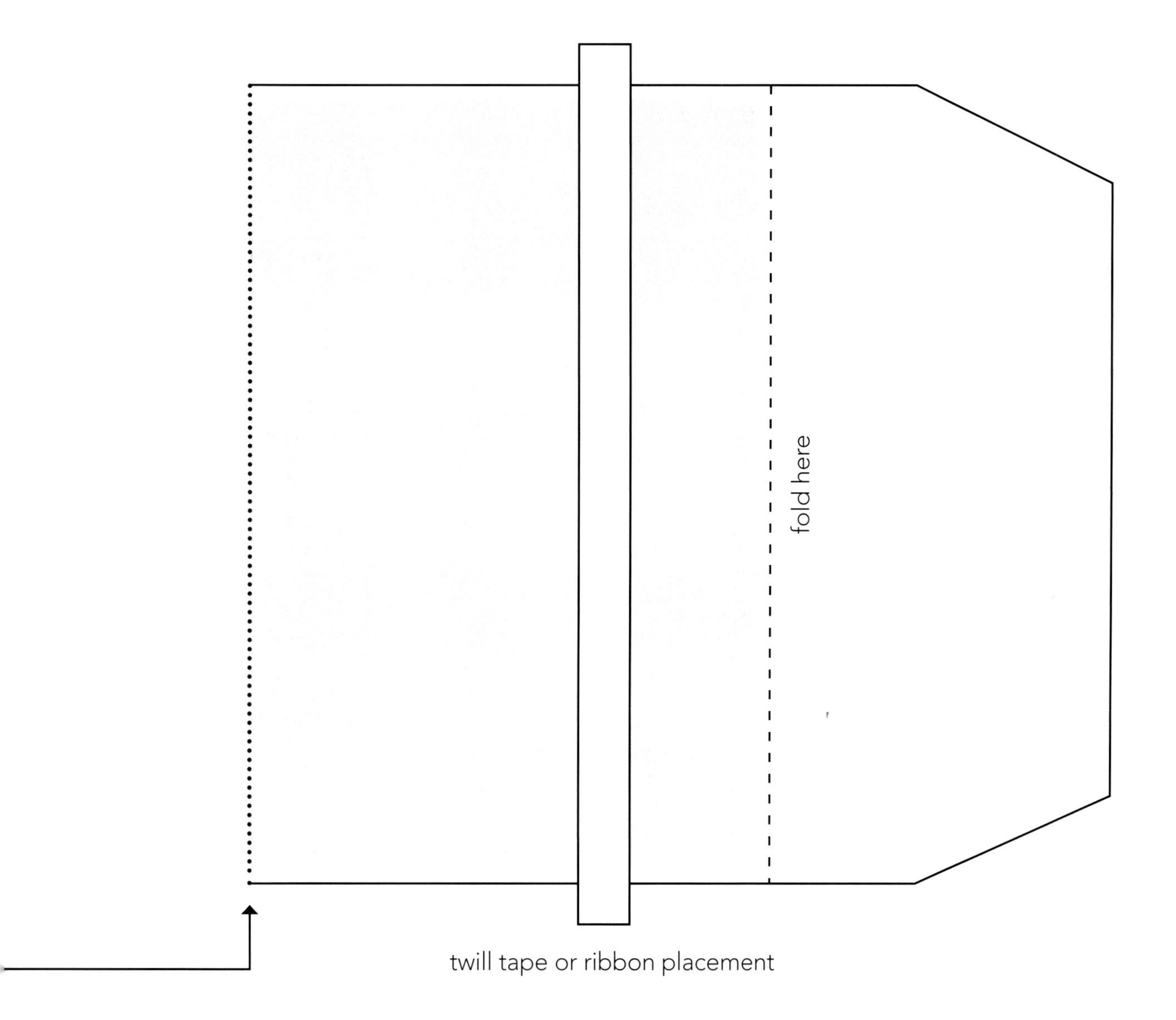
fold here
twill tape or ribbon placement

VIKING

Published by the Penguin Group
Penguin Group (Australia)
250 Camberwell Road, Camberwell, Victoria 3124, Australia
(a division of Pearson Australia Group Pty Ltd)
New York Toronto London Dublin
New Delhi Auckland Johannesburg

Penguin Books Ltd, Registered Offices: 80 Strand, London, WC2R 0RL, England

First published by Penguin Group (Australia), 2011

10 9 8 7 6 5 4 3 2 1

All props supplied by Nest Studio, Amy Prior, Umbrella Prints and Penguin Books.

All fabric by Umbrella Prints www.umbrellaprints.com.au.

Cover and text design by Marley Flory and Claire Tice © Penguin Group (Australia)
Art by Lily Brice
Illustrations by Marley Flory
Photography by Paul Nelson
Colour separation by Splitting Image P/L, Clayton, Victoria
Typeset in 12/18 pt Chaparral Pro Regular by Post Pre-press Group, Brisbane
Printed and bound in China by 1010 Printing International Limited

National Library of Australia
Cataloguing-in-Publication data:

Schwerdt, Carly
Little Artists Handmade
ISBN: 978 0670073573
1. Handicraft
2. Handicraft for children

745.5

penguin.com.au